"Dr. Buechler presents Fromm's thinking from the perspective of her own therapeutic work and experience, which is a unique and outstanding way of revealing Fromm's topicality. A very instructive book."

Dr. Rainer Funk, *Director of the Erich Fromm Institute Tübingen, Germany*

"In this work, Sandra Buechler invites us to get to know Erich Fromm in depth. Fromm's work exerts an extraordinary, sharp, and decisive influence on psychotherapists, through his emphasis on treatment's ethics, its context, sense of purpose, and the social meaning of any psychotherapeutic act. Buechler perfectly captures and transmits the nuances of Fromm's writing as it influences her own clinical practice."

Alejandro Ávila-Espada, *Honorary Chair of the Institute of Relational Psychotherapy, Madrid, Spain*

"Sandra Buechler has provided us yet another treasure: a profound yet personal look at the life, work, and influence of sociologist/psychoanalyst Erich Fromm, a front-row singer in what she often calls her 'internal chorus.' She presents him as humanist and true multi-disciplinarian, as the biophilic lover and chooser of life for which he always advocated, as clinician and philosopher. She shows how timely, and yet timeless in a Shakespearean sense, were his concerns, as we too stand before and within a fragile yet common world, full of too much indifference. Choose life, choose love, he proclaims, as does Sandra Buechler."

Donna M. Orange, *PhD, PsyD. NYU Postdoctoral Program in Psychoanalysis and Psychotherapy; Institute for the Psychoanalytic Study of Subjectivity*

Erich Fromm

In this illuminating volume, Sandra Buechler introduces Erich Fromm's groundbreaking contributions to psychoanalysis, sociology, philosophy, political action, and social criticism.

Buechler explores how Fromm's thinking and interdisciplinary vision are able to frame discussions of dilemmas in contemporary society. She offers a comprehensive biography of Fromm, before delving into his role as analyst, author, activist, sociologist, and philosopher. From her own experience as a psychoanalyst and testimonies from Fromm's many ardent followers, Buechler highlights Fromm's capacity to inspire. She considers how Fromm's writing equips students, beginning clinicians and more experienced professionals to understand what can give meaning to their efforts on behalf of troubled individuals, their riven communities, and the wider world.

Assuming no prior knowledge of Fromm's work, this book offers students in clinical and social psychology, sociology, and philosophy a vital insight into his theoretical contributions. It will also be of interest to psychoanalysts, psychologists, and social workers.

Sandra Buechler is a Training and Supervising Analyst at the William Alanson White Institute, USA. Her many books include *Making a Difference in Patients' Lives* (2008), which won the Gradiva award, *Still Practicing: The Heartaches and Joys of a Clinical Career* (2012), *Understanding and Treating Patients in Clinical Psychoanalysis: Lessons from Literature* (2015), and *Psychoanalytic Approaches to Problems in Living,* (Routledge, 2019).

Routledge Introductions to Contemporary Psychoanalysis

Aner Govrin, Ph.D. Series Editor
Yael Peri Herzovich, Ph.D. Executive Editor
Itamar Ezer Assistant Editor

"Routledge Introductions to Contemporary Psychoanalysis" is one of the prominent psychoanalytic publishing ventures of our day. It will comprise dozens of books that will serve as concise introductions dedicated to influential concepts, theories, leading figures, and techniques in psychoanalysis covering every important aspect of psychoanalysis.

The length of each book is fixed at 40,000 words.

The series' books are designed to be easily accessible to provide informative answers in various areas of psychoanalytic thought. Each book will provide updated ideas on topics relevant to contemporary psychoanalysis – from the unconscious and dreams, projective identification and eating disorders, through neuropsychoanalysis, colonialism, and spiritual-sensitive psychoanalysis. Books will also be dedicated to prominent figures in the field, such as Melanie Klein, Jaque Lacan, Sandor Ferenczi, Otto Kernberg, and Michael Eigen.

Not serving solely as an introduction for beginners, the purpose of the series is to offer compendiums of information on particular topics within different psychoanalytic schools. We ask authors to review a topic but also address the readers with their own personal views and contribution to the specific chosen field. Books will make intricate ideas comprehensible without compromising their complexity.

We aim to make contemporary psychoanalysis more accessible to both clinicians and the general educated public.

Aner Govrin – Editor

Erich Fromm: A Contemporary Introduction
Sandra Buechler

Erich Fromm

A Contemporary Introduction

Sandra Buechler

LONDON AND NEW YORK

First published 2025
by Routledge
4 Park Square, Milton Park, Abingdon, Oxon OX14 4RN

and by Routledge
605 Third Avenue, New York, NY 10158

Routledge is an imprint of the Taylor & Francis Group, an informa business

Designed cover image: Michal Heiman, Asylum 1855–2020, The Sleeper (video, psychoanalytic sofa and Plate 34), exhibition view, Herzliya Museum of Contemporary Art, 2017

British Library Cataloguing in Publication Data
A catalogue record for this book is available from the British Library

Library of Congress Cataloging-in-Publication Data
A catalog record has been requested for this book

ISBN: 978-1-032-69351-4 (hbk)
ISBN: 978-1-032-61343-7 (pbk)
ISBN: 978-1-032-69352-1 (ebk)

DOI: 10.4324/9781032693521

Typeset in Times New Roman
by Taylor & Francis Books

I dedicate this work to Griffin, Phoebe, Isaac, Eva, their parents, and my late husband, George

Contents

Acknowledgments

I would like to express my gratitude to Aner Govrin and Yael Peri Herzovich for their invitation to contribute to their series, *Routledge Introductions to Contemporary Psychoanalysis.* I also want to thank Kristopher Spring for his enormously valuable assistance in the preparation of the manuscript.

My personal analysts, supervisors, teachers, colleagues, and friends at the William Alanson White Institute (co-founded by Erich Fromm) furthered my study of Fromm's valuable insights. My peer group (Mark Blechner, Richard Gartner, John O'Leary, Annie Rosen, and Robert Watson) has sustained my spirit for over 40 years. I am eternally grateful for their unwavering support, as well as the contributions of the many analysands and supervisees who have helped me develop the perspective reflected in this book.

I am also profoundly grateful for the heroic efforts of Rainer Funk, Fromm's last research assistant, who has contributed enormously to keeping Fromm's legacy alive, through his voluminous translations, publications, and chairmanship of the International Erich Fromm Society, among many other activities. Rainer's dedication has inspired a generation of Fromm scholars. No words adequately capture my profound respect and personal gratitude for his generosity and generativity.

Introduction
Why Fromm Now?[1]

> "Today it is not Baal and Astarte but the deification of the state and of power in authoritarian countries and the deification of the machine and of success in our own culture which threaten the most precious spiritual possessions of man."
>
> (Fromm, 1950, pp. 118–119)

Remarkably, this statement was written over 70 years ago. I believe it is just as pertinent today as it was then. What do we make of that?

It is said of Shakespeare that he was both of his own time and for all time (Garber, 2004). His plays meaningfully commented on issues alive in the late 16th and early 17th century, but they have also resonated with concerns in subsequent eras. In this book, I argue that a similar claim can be made for the work of Erich Fromm. Like Shakespeare, he captured the timeless as well as the culturally and temporally specific. Fromm's work spanned the fields of sociology, psychoanalysis, philosophy, ethics, theology, anthropology, neurophysiology, and political activism. Few others have had as wide a lens. Like some of the finest scholars of all ages, Fromm was not beholden to any one field's language or fundamental axioms but, rather, only to the search for truths. In each field, he had an insider's sophistication and an outsider's capacity for critical appraisal.

We might take the continuing relevance of Fromm's thinking as evidence that some dilemmas are fundamental to the human condition. Perhaps, again, Shakespeare provides a key when, in

DOI: 10.4324/9781032693521-1

the voice of his character, Hamlet, he urges actors to "… hold, as 'twere the mirror up to Nature to show Virtue her feature, Scorn her own image, and the very age and body of the time his form and pressure" (2016, pp. 327–328).

Rather than attempt to summarize Fromm's vast contributions, I isolate some of his central concepts and comment on their contemporary relevance, as well as their influence on my own thinking, writing, and clinical practice.

Calling Fromm a public intellectual, Paul Roazen (1996) lauds his courage and "responsible outspokenness" (p. 452), which, he declares, should be a beacon to us all. I agree. Each chapter of the present book highlights one of the ways Fromm can still serve as a beacon to us all.

I come to the study of Fromm from a psychoanalytic perspective. Fromm has been a guiding light for me for over half a century. I first read him as an undergraduate in the 1960s with no awareness of the ongoing role his work would play in my professional development. Fromm appeals to much more than just my intellect. He inspires my passionate longing for a healthier society. He prompts dedication to helping patients reach for more life, one therapeutic hour at a time. He fires up the potential freedom fighter and energizes advocacy for humanistic values.

I (Buechler, 2004) have always believed that those whose lives have purpose can best bear difficult circumstances. Fromm supplies the clinician, researcher, student, and curious reader with persuasive reasons why we should expend effort to fight on behalf of the life force (biophilia, in Fromm's terms) in whatever ways we can.

I hope readers come away from this book with a clear sense of why I would argue that we need Fromm today, as much as ever before.

At the outset, I would like to acknowledge that my allocation of Fromm's concepts into chapters is somewhat arbitrary. For example, I discuss Fromm's concept of "social character" in Chapter 2 ("Fromm the Sociologist"). I believe it belongs there, but it also could be placed in the chapter on Fromm as a philosopher or Fromm as a clinician. So as not to be too repetitious, I have assigned it to the second chapter, although it is a concept that is key to all of his thinking.

Each of the six chapters that follow this introductory section deals with a facet of Fromm's prolific career. After a brief biographical sketch, I address his work as a sociologist, political activist, philosopher, clinician, author, and mentor.

In addition to these activities, Fromm was instrumental in the founding of the William Alanson White Institute in New York, the Mexican Psychoanalytic Institute, and the International Federation of Psychoanalytic Societies. His personal influence on a generation of analysts was documented in an edited volume (Cortina & Maccoby, 1996). Of particular interest is the body of work by Dr. Rainer Funk, Fromm's last research assistant, who beautifully articulated the impact of Fromm on his own life and work (Funk, 2019).

Throughout this book, I draw on my own experience of being inspired by Fromm's writing. As a beginning clinician and throughout the phases of my career, Fromm has given me a theoretical ballast. In a chapter of *Clinical Values: Emotions that Guide Psychoanalytic Treatment*, (Buechler, 2004), I suggested that reading Fromm can contribute to the clinician's stamina and help us tolerate the inevitable difficulty of the work and the confusion and doubt that can especially plague the beginning therapist. I expand on this point in the eighth chapter of this book. Fromm can facilitate our feeling a sense of mission about our work, a feeling that we are fighting on behalf of life itself, a sensation of being centered and whole. I suggested that each clinician needs an "internal chorus" of mentors to internally "consult" during stressful moments in clinical practice. Fromm has always been a prominent member of my own "internal chorus."

In a recent publication, Funk and Lechhab (2022) discuss applications of Fromm's thinking to current interpersonal, intrapersonal, and societal dilemmas. Years ago, Fromm (1986) gave an interview which mentioned some of his criticisms of society, as he experienced it then. It seems worthwhile to speculate on what he might have thought about the challenges we face today. The ninth chapter of the present book more fully explores his relevance to contemporary problems. Briefly, Fromm described trends that were obvious to him in twentieth century society and remain highly relevant in the current climate. I do not think Fromm would be at all surprised at the ways that we worship technology, the threats that products of our own invention will take control away from us, and the alienation, polarization, distrust, hypocrisy, commodification, and societal disintegration that we suffer. I imagine he would be sad to see that we still live in fear of nuclear war and environmental disaster, and that we glorify our own nation at the expense of others. Certainly, Fromm would be disturbed by the rise of fascistic, narcissistic leaders in various parts of the world. He would see us as still fostering hatred of the stranger, the "other," the immigrant, whose human commonality with ourselves we so easily deny. With sorrow but not surprise, he would observe our willingness to "escape" our freedom. I think he would reflect that we are still unable to create a society that operates according to humanistic values. He might ask why we have not moved forward in the more than 40 years since his death. He would ask psychoanalysts why we do not engage more in significant political issues. He would wonder why we have not advanced in our ability to bridge disciplines. I think Fromm would be especially disheartened at the lack of respect for truth that has seeped into every area of our lives, blurring reality and sowing seeds of cynicism and disrespect of expertise, evidence, and scientific inquiry. Fromm would ask us what we still care about, and what kind of legacy we want to leave, for our own children and future generations. In every part of this book, I encourage myself, and the reader, to ask the same questions.

Finally, I offer a brief personal statement of my relationship to Fromm's thinking, as it has evolved over more than half a century of reading, writing, and working clinically. No doubt others would understand his concepts and evaluate their significance differently. This book presents a highly selective, personal expression of his influence on my theoretical framework, clinical practice, and core beliefs as a human being. My hope is that the reader goes on to explore Fromm's writing, and that this helps them refine their own theoretical and clinical stance.

Note

1 Unless otherwise indicated, all biographical information is from Burston (1991), Cortina and Maccoby (1996), and Funk (2000, 2019).

References

Buechler, S. (2004). *Clinical values: Emotions that guide psychoanalytic treatment*. The Analytic Press.

Burston, D. (1991). *The legacy of Erich Fromm*. Harvard University Press.

Cortina, M. & Maccoby, M. (Eds) (1996). *A prophetic analyst: Erich Fromm's contribution to psychoanalysis*. Jason Aronson.

Fromm, E. (1950). *Psychoanalysis and religion*. Vail-Ballou Press, Inc.

Fromm, E. (1986). In the name of life: A portrait through dialogue. In *For the love of life* (pp. 88–116). The Free Press.

Funk, R. (2000). *Erich Fromm: His life and ideas*. Continuum.

Funk, R. (2019). *Life itself is an art: The life and work of Erich Fromm*. Bloomsbury Academic.

Funk, R. & Lechhab, H. (2022). *The significance of Erich Fromm for the present*. Zeuys Books.

Garber, M. (2004). *Shakespeare after all*. Anchor Books.

Roazen, P. (1996). Erich Fromm's courage. In M. Cortina & M. Maccoby (Eds), *A prophetic analyst: Erich Fromm's contribution to psychoanalysis* (pp. 427–453). Jason Aronson.

Shakespeare, W. (2016). Hamlet. In A. Thompson & N. Taylor (Eds), *The Arden Shakespeare*. Bloomsbury Publishing Company.

Part I

Fromm the Person

Chapter 1

Brief Biography of Fromm's Life[1]

When I meet a new patient, I generally ask them to tell me about "the situation you were born into." This question is also a statement. Each of us was born into a situation we did not create. This context will have a significant impact on our lives.

If someone could choose where and when to be born so as to be sensitized to the imprint of society on the individual, the straddling of disparate worldviews, the influence of irrational forces, and the universality of the human predicament of needing both freedom and belonging, they might choose the circumstances of Fromm's birth.

Erich Seligmann Fromm was born in Frankfurt am Main on March 23, 1900, the only child of Jewish parents, Naphtali and Rosa. His adolescence was deeply affected by the brutality of the First World War, and his adult life was profoundly impacted by the unfathomable tragedy of the Second World War. I cannot imagine more impressive demonstrations of both the power of irrational forces and the imprint of the social world on individual development. Erich had minority status as a Jew in Germany and, in a sense, as an only child in a large family of adults. Naphtali hoped Erich would become a rabbi, but his own position was head of a chapter of the Hermann Cohen Society, a group devoted to the study of a Neo-Kantian philosopher. As a child, Erich studied with rabbinical scholars, but, eventually, his intellect ranged beyond any one field to encompass sociology, psychoanalysis, politics, history, anthropology, neurology, and Zen Buddhism. Fromm bridged a Marxist philosophy of values with a psychoanalytic study of the unconscious. He brought

DOI: 10.4324/9781032693521-3

together the teachings of Buddhists with the findings of psychological and sociological research. Integrating insights from multiple perspectives was a pursuit he raised to an art form. We might speculate about how his life circumstances facilitated having one foot in each of many fields, but, regardless of this, it is clear that part of Fromm's enormous contribution is his ability to be a profession's "insider" and "outsider" at one and the same time. In both sociology and psychoanalysis, he had an insider's profound understanding, an outsider's capacity to critique, and a truth-seeker's willingness to engage in controversy.

My way of thinking is that Fromm did something that many other great scholars are also able to accomplish: He turned what could be a handicap into an advantage. Just as Freud took a potentially negative experience (the abrupt departure of his patient, Dora) and *made it into an opportunity* to further his understanding of the treatment relationship, Fromm made his personal familiarity with being an "outsider" stand him in good stead in his professional life. Funk (2000) quotes Fromm as saying, "I felt quite at home neither in the world I lived in, nor in the old world of traditions" (p. 10). Erich, the Jew in Germany, became Dr. Erich Fromm, the sociologist/psychoanalyst. With his knowledge of sociology, he could approach psychoanalysis differently from other analysts, and with his background in psychoanalysis, he could forge a new sociological perspective. While he was "othered" by some in both fields, he found ways to use his multiple allegiances to enrich his work as a clinician and author. But, of course, his outsider status came at a price, as we will see shortly. What I want to emphasize here is this capacity to make *use* of his position, rather than allowing it to disqualify him, at least in his own eyes. Similarly, Funk quotes Fromm as saying that "having grown up in a very neurotic family" allowed him to become "more aware of what the irrationalities of human behavior really represent" (p. 16). Once again, a potential drawback is transformed into an asset. It reminds me of how science frequently advances by studying the experimental results that "fail" to conform to expectations. Serendipitous findings can be reframed into opportunities for further inquiry. I think this attitude embodies the curiosity and courage of the intrepid explorer.

Fromm's biography can be taken to exemplify another recurring feature of many psychoanalytic pioneers: using personal experience as a resource for discovering generalizable theoretical premises. From the crucible of his childhood with a father who anxiously restricted him, Fromm became a vigorous champion of psychological freedom (Funk, 2000). At a profound level, he understood what it meant to be hampered in the quest for full self-development. From a mother who sharply distinguished between "us" (her own family) and "them" (the Fromm's), he took lessons about the conflictual impact of "us vs. them" divisions. Fromm fought passionately for tolerance and against all forms of "group narcissism" (Funk, 2019, p. 121). While it would be reductionistic to interpret Fromm's theoretical positions as merely products of his own childhood, I think it can be argued that his personal experiences planted seeds and, perhaps, contributed to the passion of his convictions.

I think it is inevitable that the *story of our early lives coheres around beliefs constructed later.* Thus, Fromm *remembered* the teacher who voiced opinions contrary to prevailing prowar sentiments (Funk, 2000). Would he have recalled this moment if his later life had bent toward patriotic fervor? Of course, we can never know, but as it stood the experience at 14 of an independent-minded teacher was indelible.

Rather than patriotic fervor, the young Fromm developed strong feelings about the Old Testament prophets. It has been said about the prophets that they lived in accordance with what they preached and spoke the truth, even if it risked their imprisonment, ostracism, or death. I can think of no better template for some of the values Fromm held in later adulthood. In my own work (Buechler, 2004), I have thought of this quality as integrity and have considered it imperative for the clinician (as well, of course, as the rest of us).

Early influences on Fromm's intellectual and spiritual development included Rabbi Nobel, whose teaching brought together Hasidic and Enlightenment strands. Fromm took up the study of the Talmud with Dr. Salman Baruch Rabinkow. Interestingly, when still quite young, Fromm had to deal with a clash of values, as his opposition to nationalism crystallized. This motivated his resignation from a Zionist youth organization in 1923. It would not be the last time Fromm's passionate beliefs had an interpersonal cost. His extraordinarily integrating mind brought differing perspectives together, but, sometimes, his belief in living what you preach necessitated choosing one over the other. What prevailed is Fromm's strong attachment to the humanistic vision of One Man, that is, the idea (developed in Fromm, 1962) that, while our customs differ, the human substance is the same throughout the world and throughout time. As we will see in other chapters, this fundamental idea informed Fromm's sociological, philosophical, and clinical work.

After taking courses in law, philosophy, history, and economics, Fromm pursued doctoral studies under the supervision of the sociologist Alfred Weber (brother of Max Weber). Eventually, Fromm earned his PhD with a study of the social functions of Jewish Law. I think it is noteworthy that Fromm's interest was in the way the law promoted social cohesion. I imagine this topic enabled Fromm to bring his prior interest in biblical scholarship together with his growing awareness of social and psychological issues. To integrate complicated bodies of work took a scholar able to be both an "insider" who understands fundamental premises and, at the same time, an "outsider" who can recognize gaps that could be filled by insights from another line of thought. Fromm's powerful mind and diligent pursuit of knowledge enabled him to be that scholar.

Fromm's early adult experiences also included friendship, professional projects, and eventual marriage to the psychoanalyst Frieda Fromm-Reichmann. But not long after their marriage, tuberculosis forced him to spend time on his own recuperating in Davos. Then came events in 1933, a fork in the road for his country and for Fromm personally. Hitler came to power, Fromm's father died, and, in 1934, Fromm moved to the US. He was unable to persuade his mother to leave Germany until Kristallnacht. After two years in England, she came to New York, living there until she died of cancer in 1959.

Fromm lost many relatives to the concentration camps. Roger Frie (2022), a psychoanalyst and historian, has made extensive study of the effect of the war on Fromm's life and work. Frie

(2019) and Funk (2000) tell the heart-rending story of family members of Fromm who perished. Some (such as Fromm's aunt, Sophie Englander) apparently held on to hope for future family reunions. Tragically, they were not to be.

I think of Fromm's intellectual development as a rich tapestry or musical composition. The theme of the life of the spirit took hold in early life, at first with an interest in the Jewish religion, much later in Buddhism, but always expressed in valuing nourishing the soul. Then came the theme of the intrinsically interpersonal nature of the human being and the imprint of society on the individual. Then psychoanalysis, and the life of the unconscious, added richness and depth to the design. As might be said of many lives, the overall pattern is much clearer in retrospect than it could have been at the time of its creation. Not everyone has the intellect to retain such diverse influences. Not everyone has the psychological strength to withstand being both an insider and outsider in several fields. Not everyone has the courage to stand up for what they believe in, when encountering severe criticism and, even worse, disregard. Fromm was one person who was equipped to do all of this.

Each of these threads has an interpersonal history in Fromm's life. His interest in the religious and non-religious life of the soul had its beginnings in his family but was greatly enhanced by teachers who provided inspiring ethical role models as well as intellectual input. Fromm's sociological studies were partially motivated by a profound need to understand better the meaning of cataclysmic world events and furthered by influential mentors, such as Alfred Weber. His study of psychoanalysis was nurtured by his friend, and later wife, Frieda Reichmann. It was through her that he met many other analysts who had a significant impact on his development as a clinician and theoretician. Each thread contributes to the power and lasting influence of his thinking. At least for me, I can say that without any one of these threads I would be less devoted to studying his work. I feel that it is their combination that makes Fromm so relevant to the present moment in history (see Chapter 9 for more about this). Today, technology challenges us to meet its advances without losing our connection to the spiritual values that have guided us in the past.

Polarizing group processes and political factions force us to examine the relationship between the individual and society. Incidences of horrendous violence demand that we examine human motivations and, especially, their destructive expressions, as well as the life forces that can prevail. Fromm addresses all of these issues in ways that make him both incredibly prescient and relevant.

After Fromm obtained his doctorate in 1925, his friendship with Frieda Reichmann, a psychiatrist 11 years his senior, led him to the study of Freudian psychoanalysis. Together, they created a "therapeuticum" where Jewish patients could gain awareness of unconscious experience. They married in 1926. Fromm pursued psychoanalytic insight through personal analysis with Wilhelm Wittenberg, by attending lectures, getting to know Georg Groddeck, Karen Horney, and Sándor Ferenczi, and, in 1928, completing his psychoanalytic training with Hanns Sachs at the Karl Abraham Institute in Berlin.

The early 1930s brought another significant change. Fromm fell ill with tuberculosis and moved to Switzerland to be treated. Then, having decided to separate from Frieda, Fromm accepted an invitation from Karen Horney to lecture in Chicago. Some of Fromm's sociological and psychoanalytic ideas coalesced into an essay, "The Dogma of Christ," in 1930. Fromm's theoretical development and prolific output as an author is the subject of a separate chapter, but here I mention that his capacity to integrate ideas from religion, sociology, and psychology was already evident in this publication.

The bout with tuberculosis, and his recuperation in Switzerland, can be seen as another example of Fromm's capacity to make productive use of unfortunate circumstances. He used the time to develop his sociopolitical ideas, studying (among others) the work of Johann Jacob Bachofen, who wrote about differences between matriarchal and patriarchal societies.

Fromm's relationship with Max Horkheimer and the Frankfurt Institute for Social Research, and his development of the concept of the authoritarian personality, began in the 1930s. Both the Institute and Fromm himself made several geographical moves but ended up in New York.

Not for the first or last time the ideas of one thinker (Bacho-fen) led Fromm to critique the theories of another (Freud). During his recovery in Davos, he made contact with Ernst Schachtel, among many other influential thinkers, and was visited by Herbert Marcuse and Frieda. By then, Fromm was playing a significant role in the development of the Institute for Social Research. Both the Institute and Fromm relocated to New York in 1934. His relationship with Karen Horney grew closer, and he anticipated productive years of collaboration with Institute colleagues, who showed great interest in his thinking. However, repeated bouts of illness interfered in some of his work until 1939. Along with the hardships of ill health, Fromm had to bear disastrous political news from Germany, Spain, and Moscow.

Extreme tribulations tested Fromm in this period. In addition to the worsening political situation and his own ill health, Fromm had to deal with economic challenges, as he struggled to help his mother emigrate. In a telling letter to Horkheimer, Fromm reflects:

> Sometimes, during these weeks, it has seemed more than doubtful to me, if under the circumstances, it was still worth holding on to one's life as it were "by force," through doctors, medicines-and the inner will to live. But the feeling "I can make it" stayed more prominent...we have a responsibility as individuals not to give in. Besides this there is satisfaction in knowing that, even though we might get physically crushed by the steamroller of historical events, we will stay intact spiritually and morally.
>
> (Funk, 2000, p. 86)

As I hear it, Fromm once again forged a significant outlook on the human condition from his challenging circumstances. The strength of the will to live, the importance of *how we meet* life's tribulations, and the meaningfulness of spiritual and moral forces are succinctly expressed in this moving personal statement. To me, it is no wonder that his work inspired so many and continues to do so more than 40 years after his death.

It is with sorrow that I review the deterioration of Fromm's relationship with the Institute for Social Research. I am sad because there have been so many schisms in the history of my field, psychoanalysis, with theoretical differences as at least part of their basis. If only we could look at our colleagues' beliefs with the same openness and curiosity that we expect of ourselves when we are with our patients!

As I understand it, at the heart of the break between Fromm and the Institute was Fromm's development of a theoretical framework that emphasized social conditions, and not just libidinal instincts. Funk (2000) quotes a letter Fromm wrote as saying that "The task seems to me to be to understand the structure of character and instincts as a result of adaptation to the given social conditions and not as a product of the erogenous zones" (p. 93).

I will not try to adjudicate the many aspects of the conflict between Fromm and the Institute, except to say that whatever part Fromm's position played means that, not for the first or last time, Fromm suffered ostracism for his passionate convictions. I hope we can take from this episode a strengthened determination to embrace differences of all kinds, in colleagues and in the wider world, and treat the "other" with respect, as providing an opportunity for learning and growth.

Even though plagued with repeated episodes of tuberculosis, Fromm's thinking evolved in the 1930s, and in 1941 he published the widely influential book *Escape from Freedom* (a later chapter will discuss this further). Fromm was refining his view of a *dialectic* relationship between our biological necessities and the societally determined conditions in which they must be satisfied. Essentially, Fromm would not back down from this conviction. Studying the effects of the culture, Fromm developed his view of social character types (further discussed in subsequent chapters), eventually including not just the authoritarian character but also the marketing character and other categories. In other words, if we grow up in a society that places a premium on success in the marketplace, we are likely to internalize this value, and it will help shape how we live our lives. This fundamental position informed his extensive research efforts and prolific writing from the 1930s on. Sadly, the rift between Fromm and the Institute only widened and resulted in a final break in 1939.

According to an old saying, when one door closes, another opens. That certainly was true for Fromm. As his relationship with the Institute for Social Research deteriorated, he was invited by H. S. Sullivan to join in the activities of the Washington School of Psychiatry. Like Fromm, Sullivan believed that humans are inherently social beings and that treatment should center on the way the patient relates interpersonally. My take on this is that, in the long run, it was bound to be more fruitful for Fromm to bring his background in sociology to Interpersonal psychoanalysis than it was for him to try to bring his version of psychoanalysis to the sociologists at the Institute for Social Research. In the 1930s an interdisciplinary spirit reigned in the new Interpersonal school of psychiatry and psychoanalysis. For example, in the first four issues (1938) of the journal *Psychiatry*, articles on sociology, anthropology, philosophy, political science, law, economics, biology, psychiatry, and psychoanalysis were published side by side. Sullivan invited Fromm to an enterprise heartily welcoming what he could contribute. Along with Sullivan, Clara Thompson, Frieda Fromm-Reichmann, and others, Fromm was able to put his stamp on both the Washington School of Psychiatry and its New York branch, the William Alanson White Institute. My cohort of candidates in psychoanalytic training at the W. A. White Institute between 1979 and 1983 thought of Sullivan and Fromm as our two most important forbears. While not without its own conflicts, in this newly emerging field Fromm found an intellectual home base, and in *Psychiatry* he found a new venue for publications.

It was in this context that Fromm more fully developed his clinical approach, which is the subject of two later chapters in this volume. Fromm was a substantial influence in my own analytic training at the W. A. White Institute. My Training Analyst, Rose Spiegel, MD, and my first Analytic Supervisor, Ralph Crowley, MD, frequently referenced Fromm. From them and from many others who knew Fromm, I got the impression that he was remarkably inspiring. His unusually strong effect on a generation of clinicians deserves its own chapter, so I discuss it separately. There I speculate about how he evoked a loyalty that is still evident in the many activities of the International Erich Fromm Society, which was founded in 1985 and is presently a growing and thriving organization.

In his extremely popular book *Escape from Freedom* (1941), Fromm found a wide audience for his thinking about the authoritarian characters who lead and follow in fascistic regimes. In many chapters I note how, sadly, these issues are still timely.

Besides this career success, Fromm also established a new marriage, to Henny Gurland, who, together with her son, had fled from the Nazis. In the 1940s Fromm's busy career included teaching at the New School for Social Research in New York, Bennington College in Vermont, and as a lecturer at Yale. Along with his many lectures, Fromm wrote several books in this period, as mentioned in the chapter on his contributions as an author.

The end of the 1940s brought Fromm the sorrow of Henny's severe arthritic pain, their move to Mexico in the hope that the climate would ease her suffering, and Henny's death in 1950. Fromm remained in Mexico until 1973, where he played an important part in the development of psychoanalytic training in that country.

As Fromm's thinking developed, he focused on the universality of our fundamental humanness, which is represented in the unconscious. Over the years, an interest in Zen Buddhism added to Fromm's personal meditative practice and his psychoanalytic perspective. The 1950s brought love center stage, with the publication of his extremely popular book, *The Art of Loving* (1956), and with his marriage to Annis Freeman in 1953. All accounts (Funk, 2000) suggest that Fromm's theoretical belief in an active, center-to-center form of loving guided his personal relationship with Annis.

Fromm's views about love have been extremely meaningful to me. In *The Art of Loving*, he describes its challenges, including the need to actively practice loving and enter into it fully. I devoted the first chapter of *Psychoanalytic Approaches to Problems in Living* (Buechler, 2019) to the idea that the relatively secure person has a capacity for bearing aloneness as well as a capacity to invest in relationships. I expressed this by saying that I think "…the capacities for solitude and relationship are twins, conceived in the benign environment created by our first love" (p. 18). I credited Fromm with inspiring many of the ideas in this book, calling him the most influential of the voices of analysts I have internalized in my own "internal chorus" of wise clinicians.

Another of Fromm's accomplishments had a direct effect on my career. He played a major role in the establishment of the International Federation of Psychoanalytic Societies in 1962. The IFPS is a vibrant group of analytic societies that meets every two years in different member countries. Its theoretical and cultural diversity and warm collegial atmosphere have been a source of wonderful professional opportunities and personal friendships for me.

Fromm's direct involvement in politics took several forms, including cofounding SANE ("National Committee for a Sane Nuclear Policy"), raising the issue of disarmament in letters to religious leaders and politicians and actively campaigning for Eugene McCarthy in his bid to become the president of the US.

In Mexico, aside from his involvement in psychoanalytic training, Fromm also devoted time to field research, and, with Michael Maccoby, published *Social Character in a Mexican Village: A Sociopsychoanalytic Study* (1970). This evolved into a line of research, carried out in several countries, on the relationship between economic and social structure and character patterns.

In the last decade of his life, Fromm continued to refine his perspective on human motivation, publishing *The Anatomy of Human Destructiveness* in 1973. In a sense, Fromm searched his whole life for a greater understanding of the causes of destructiveness. The theory he developed is that the primary tendency in human beings is biophilic. Destructive tendencies are an outgrowth of failed or blocked life forces. I take up the vast clinical implications of this viewpoint separately, but here I want to mention how closely it resembles a thread in my own work. Coming from a background in emotion theory (Izard, 1972, 1977), I (Buechler, 2008) focused on the balance of the positive and negative emotions as pivotal to the texture of human experience and as key to therapeutic approaches. The significance of a balance is prominent in Fromm's thinking and emotion theory, and, retrospectively, I see my own framework as partially derived from both.

Fromm had his first heart attack in 1966, which interrupted all his activities. In 1974 Erich and Annis moved to Locarno, Switzerland. That was also the time when Rainer Funk became his assistant and began decades of devotion to Fromm scholarship. In his later years, Fromm worked on a statement of two ways of life, which became his book *To Have or To Be?* (1976). The continuing relevance of this distinction will be explored in the last chapter of this volume.

In his last years, Fromm continued political activities, symposia, lectures, and varied professional and personal contacts, although he suffered from gallstones and three more heart attacks. The last of them, on March 18, 1980, was fatal.

Fromm often mentioned the phrase from Deuteronomy (30:15–20): "Now choose life, so that you and your children may live." I would select these words to express the central message he conveyed in his writing but, perhaps even more tellingly, in how he connected with others, stood up for his beliefs, and cultivated his own inner life.

Rainer Funk, the literary executor of the Erich Fromm Estate and the editor of the multivolume publication of Fromm's complete works, is the most comprehensive and authoritative source of information about Fromm's life and writing. In English, aside from his book, Erich Fromm: His Life and Ideas (Continuum, 2000), Funk also contributed a volume that integrates Fromm's life experience with his conceptual output, Life Itself Is an Art: The Life and Work of Erich Fromm (Bloomsbury Academic, 2019). For additional information, see the valuable study by Jack Jacobs, The Frankfurt School, Jewish Lives, and Antisemitism (Cambridge University Press, 2015).

Note

1 Unless otherwise indicated, all biographical information is from Burston (1991), Cortina and Maccoby (1996), and Funk (2000, 2019).

References

Buechler, S. (2004). *Clinical values: Emotions that guide psychoanalytic treatment*. The Analytic Press.

Buechler, S. (2008). *Making a difference in patients' lives: Emotional experience in the therapeutic setting*. Routledge.

Buechler, S. (2019). *Psychoanalytic approaches to problems in living: Addressing life's challenges in clinical practice.* Routledge.

Burston, D. (1991). *The legacy of Erich Fromm.* Harvard University Press.

Cortina, M. & Maccoby, M. (Eds) (1996). *A prophetic analyst: Erich Fromm's contribution to psychoanalysis.* Jason Aronson.

Frie, R. (2019). Psychoanalysis, persecution and the Holocaust: Erich Fromm's life and work during the 1930s. In R. Funk & T. Kuhn (Eds), *Putting society on the couch* (pp. 70–79). International Erich Fromm Society.

Frie, R. (2022). Psychoanalysis in the shadow of fascism and genocide: Erich Fromm and the Interpersonal tradition. In R. Frie & P. Sauvayre (Eds), *Culture, politics and race in the making of interpersonal psychoanalysis: Breaking boundaries* (pp. 237–263). Routledge.

Fromm, E. (1930). The dogma of Christ. In *The dogma of Christ and other essays on religion, psychology and culture* (pp. 3–95). Holt, Rinehart & Winston.

Fromm, E. (1941). *Escape from freedom.* Farrar & Rinehart.

Fromm, E. (1956). *The art of loving.* Harper & Row.

Fromm, E. (1962). *Beyond the chains of illusion: My encounter with Marx and Freud.* Simon & Schuster.

Fromm, E. (1973). *The anatomy of human destructiveness.* Holt, Rinehart & Winston.

Fromm, E. (1976). *To have or to be?* Harper & Row.

Fromm, E. & Maccoby, M. (1970). *Social character in a Mexican village: A sociopsychoanalytic study.* Prentice-Hall.

Funk, R. (2000). *Erich Fromm: His life and ideas.* Continuum.

Funk, R. (2019). *Life itself is an art: The life and work of Erich Fromm.* Bloomsbury Academic.

Izard, C. E. (1972). *Patterns of emotion.* Academic Press.

Izard, C. E. (1977). *Human emotions.* Plenum Press.

Part II

Fromm's Multidisciplinary Career

Chapter 2

Fromm the Sociologist[1]

After being mentored in the Talmud and taking courses in law, philosophy, history, and economics, Fromm studied sociology. He earned a PhD with a dissertation on the social functions of Jewish Law. Despite these credentials, whether Fromm should be considered a sociologist has been questioned (McLaughlin, 2021, reviews the issues). Here, I focus on some of Fromm's central concepts about socio-economic forces, their effect on societal norms, and their impact on human behavior. Fromm's criticisms of some of society's influences are also discussed in the chapter on contemporary issues. In the introduction to his book, Neil McLaughlin (2021) writes of Fromm's credentials as a public sociologist. Mentioning Fromm's studies of *Marx's Concept of Man* (1961a) and *May Man Prevail?* (1961b), McLaughlin suggests that these books utilized sociological frameworks, were read by sociologists, and "warrant a close revisiting" (p. 11). While Fromm is hard to categorize into one professional frame, it is clear that he contributed to the Frankfurt Institute of Social Research and, more generally, to the sociological literature. In what follows, I describe some of his key ideas.

Social Character

This concept is fundamental to Fromm's thinking. He defined the social character as:

> that part of their character structure that is common to most members of the group. We can call this character the social

DOI: 10.4324/9781032693521-5

character...if we want to understand how human energy is channeled and operates as a productive force in a given social order, then the social character deserves our main interest... the subjective function of character for the normal person is to lead him to act according to what is necessary for him from a practical standpoint and also to give him satisfaction from his activity psychologically...by adapting himself to social conditions man develops those traits that make him desire to act as he has to act...

(1941, pp. 1–3)

In the concept of the social character, Fromm describes the impact of social conditions on individual development. They facilitate our becoming people who *want* to act in the ways our culture needs us to act. For example, if our society needs us to be consumers, we become interested in consuming. How does this happen? For Fromm, the family is society's conduit:

"[Families] transmit to the child what we may call the psychological atmosphere or the spirit of society just by being as they are—namely representatives of this very spirit. The family thus may be considered to be the psychological agent of society."

(p. 5)

As I understand it, the social character can play a significant role in our inner conflicts and interpersonal lives. In other words, if our society inculcates, let's say, prejudices that we internalize, but through our life experiences we also internalize values that are diametrically opposed to prejudice, we will be in conflict with ourselves. To me, this means that the analyst can't afford to look aside from the dictates of society, since they are likely to be a significant aspect of our patients' internal and interpersonal experience and approach to life.

In my own language, I would suggest that the internalization of the dictates of the social character theoretically could reduce the potential for *obsessive* conflicts between what we are supposed to do and what we want to do. Briefly, the typical obsessive conflict is something like "I should do 'X' but I want to do 'Y.' I don't know what to do." To the extent that the family (and other influences) have molded an individual, theoretically the child should be better able to integrate their desires with their obligations and *want* to do what society needs them to want to do. In other words, at least in the abstract, they will be able to satisfy society's requirements at the same time as they gratify their own needs. Of course, individuals vary from this theoretical abstraction.

In an empirical study of the concept of social character, Fromm and Maccoby (1970) administered interviews and projective tests to all the members of a Mexican village. The study was an exploration of the interaction of socioeconomic and characterological factors. Basically, what they concluded was that class situation had an impact on the formation of character, and, in turn, character influenced economic behavior. McLaughlin (2021) reviews the criticisms and theoretical differences spawned by this study and concludes that, despite the controversies, the Fromm and Maccoby work is "worth re-examination and building on" (p. 197). The model of participatory social research was carried forward, including, for example, in the research of Michael Maccoby, Salvador Millan, and Sonia Gojman de Millan (as described in Funk, 2000).

Frommian Character Types and Orientations

Fromm believed that different character patterns have been prevalent at various points in history and in varying socioeconomic circumstances. They include, for example, the authoritarian, marketing, and narcissistic characters. Rainer Funk (2019) has also added the ego-oriented character to the list. It is important to note that there are productive and non-productive forms of each character type.

Authoritarian Character and Orientation

Fromm investigated working-class attitudes and authoritarian character structures in Weimar Germany. McLaughlin (2021) and

Funk (2019), among others, tell the story of how Fromm was denied credit for his study, but concepts derived from it certainly informed much of his writing. Fromm refers to the authoritarian character in *Escape from Freedom* (1941), where he describes this as one who "...admires authority and tends to submit to it, but at the same time he wants to be an authority himself and have others submit to him" (p. 186). Thus, dominance and submission are a theme in all the variants of this character type, though they are expressed to different degrees. A bit later, Fromm writes: "The feature common to all authoritarian thinking is the conviction that life is determined by forces outside of man's own self, his interest, his wishes. The only possible happiness lies in the submission to these forces" (p. 194). Funk (2019) notes that dominance can be practiced toward oneself, as well as toward others, and summarizes that "In the authoritarian social character, underdevelopment of one's own powers related to the *autonomy of the individual* are most notable" (p. 100, italics in original).

Marketing Character and Orientation

The marketing character values salability, whether of goods, services, or one's own persona. Everything, including one's self-presentation, becomes a commodity in this context. Visual appearance, image, and performance are among the important variables. For example, I was once consulted by a young woman who came for treatment to get a "ten." Having no idea what that meant, I asked her what a "ten" is. Surprised that I, as a woman, would be ignorant about this, she explained that a "ten" is a man who scores ten out of ten on a scale of appearance, professional accomplishment, and other qualities. In this cultural milieu, everything and everyone is rated and up for sale. This orientation essentially creates two classes: winners and losers.

While Fromm alluded to these issues in his earlier writing, he spelled it out in detail in *Man for Himself* (1947). He described the economic functions of the market in modern society as the basis for the development of this orientation in its citizens. Simply put, Fromm explains, "The character orientation which is rooted in the experience of oneself as a commodity and of one's value as exchange value I call the marketing orientation" (p. 76).

Fromm spells out the consequences of this orientation:

> "If one feels that one's own value is not constituted primarily by the human qualities one possesses, but by one's success on a competitive market with ever-changing conditions, one's self-esteem is bound to be shaky and in constant need of confirmation by others."
>
> (p. 79)

In a statement that I hear as stressing the assumption of a role, rather than the expression of a centered sense of self, Funk (2019) writes:

> The marketing-oriented person wants to renounce anything that could distinguish his own, unique, individual personality. His inherent nature becomes alien to him, and he encounters it as a role and personality into which he slips so that he can be successful in the market. This, however, makes it impossible for him to sense his own identity as belonging to him and to experience his own individuality.
>
> (p. 105)

Advertising, publicity, social media, the internet, and so many other aspects of culture depend on (and support) marketing values.

Narcissistic Character and Orientation

In much of his writing (e.g., Fromm, 1947, 1956, 1964), Fromm distinguishes between healthy self-love and selfish narcissism; he also distinguishes between what he calls "benign" and "malignant" narcissism (1947, p. 77). In benign forms, the person takes pride in effortful work, while in the malignant forms, they are proud of attributes (something the person has, such as looks, health, or money). In a beautifully succinct statement, Fromm also describes the form of narcissism that occurs in groups:

The essence of this over-estimation of one's own position and the hate for all who differ from it is narcissism. "We" are admirable; "they" are despicable, "We" are good; "they" are evil. Any criticism of one's own doctrine is a vicious and unbearable attack; criticism of others' position is a well-meant attempt to help them return to the truth.

(p. 82)

Fromm contrasts forms of narcissism with humanism, with which he clearly identifies. All the great humanistic religions teach that it is our goal to overcome both individual and group narcissism. More generally, in all forms of individual and group narcissism, objectivity and rational judgment suffer.

One object for group and individual narcissism Fromm names is the "technique." In what I think of as an apt comment on his own culture, and a prescient description of ours, he says:

[S]cience has created a new object for narcissism—*technique*. Man's narcissistic pride in being the creator of a formerly undreamed-of world of things, the discoverer of the radio, television, atomic power, space travel, and even in being the potential destroyer of the entire globe, has given him a new object for narcissistic self-inflation.

(1964, p. 84, italics in original)

Among the attributes of "low grade" narcissism, Funk (2019) lists overestimation of self, self-centeredness, idealization of the familiar, disdain and disinterest for everything beyond the self, grandiose daydreaming, lack of empathy, striving for special status, vulnerability to criticism, depressive tendencies, inability to experience guilt, failure, and other feelings, and a striving for extreme self-sufficiency. The "strongly marked narcissistic character" is a more incapacitating form.

Funk (2019) describes another social character, the "ego orientation." For such individuals, the goal is to do everything in new and different ways. This current iteration, whose basis is technological advances, is central to the chapter on contemporary issues in the present volume.

Fromm's discussions of the effects of socio-economic forces on group and individual behavior go far beyond the brief comments offered here. More extensive discussions can be found in Fromm (1961a, 1968, 1976), Funk (1982, 2000, 2019), and McLaughlin (2021), among many others.

In his thorough, scholarly account of Fromm as a "public sociologist," McLaughlin (2021) states that the purpose of his book is to "...narrate the story of the rise, fall, and now revival of Fromm's sociology in relation to the broader scholarly literature on public sociology" (p. 3). McLaughlin refers to Fromm's "optimal marginality" (p. 51), a very felicitous term, from my perspective. He also discusses the professional advantages and pitfalls of public sociologists "on the border between the professional sociologist and celebrity intellectual" (p. 51). In my own experiences, presenting Fromm's ideas to audiences that are not familiar with his books, many are highly appreciative of his insights and their astonishing contemporary relevance. But some sociologists find him too much of a psychoanalyst, and some psychoanalysts find him too sociologically oriented. The contemporary move away from comfort with an interdisciplinary focus has been examined in a fascinating book edited by Frie and Sauvayre (2022). Sadly, among other professional groups, branches of psychoanalysis in the United States began with a firm investment in interdisciplinary thinking but, over time, became more insulated. As I see it, this has resulted in creative limitations, and the very "us" vs. "them" mentality that Fromm so eloquently fought against in the wider society. In other words, the phenomena Fromm so passionately critiqued have been (and are still) leveled against him, by his own professional associations! This reminds me of my early efforts to define the "culture" of psychoanalysis, with its mores, rules about membership, rebels, conformists, banishments, and so on (Buechler, 1988). In a sense, this iteration of an "us" vs. "them" mentality brings us to another highly significant Frommian concept, the pathology of normalcy.

Pathology of Normalcy

There are potential pitfalls in society's influence on the individual. Fromm wrote about the grave risks of a too ready willingness to fulfill society's requirements. Adaptation can be ultimately destructive if society itself is not geared toward human growth. Fromm (1955) described a "pathology" of normalcy:

> The fact that millions of people share the same vices does not make these vices virtues, the fact that they share so many errors does not make the errors to be truths, and the fact that millions of people share the same forms of mental pathology does not make these people sane.
>
> (p. 15)

Funk (2019) put it succinctly: "The pathology always consists of a socially dictated 'healthy common sense' that impedes or thwarts the psychic capacity for growth" (p. 164).

In *Psychoanalysis and Religion* (1950), Fromm is especially clear about the problem of seeing adaptation to society as a goal: "We find that according to one conception adjustment is the aim of analytic cure. By adjustment is meant a person's ability to act like the majority of people in his culture" (pp. 73). By contrast, in a second view, "the aim of therapy is not primarily adjustment but optimal development of a person's potentialities and the realization of his individuality" (p. 74). Fromm clearly endorses this second perspective, since societies can be unhealthy, so adjusting well to them might not be indicated. In Fromm's words:

> "Here the psychoanalyst is not an 'adjustment counselor' but, to use Plato's expression, the 'physician of the soul.' This view is based on the premise that there are immutable laws inherent in human nature and human functioning which operate in any given culture."
>
> (p. 74)

Just as an example, I mention my own work with many patients who had suffered from trying to adapt to society's expectations about sexual orientations. Some, pressured by their families and the attitudes of their cultures, tried to "fit in" by marrying and having children. For many, this was a disastrous and highly costly effort, in several senses. The suffering they felt can hardly be described. Of course, psychoanalysts (including Fromm) have sometimes been influenced by their culture's definitions of healthy living. We are all (including clinicians) products of our times, affected by the "social filter" (Fromm, 1962) that limits our perceptions and slants our interpretations. But I think Fromm's theories provide a valuable basis for questioning the role of societal and familial pressures on an individual's self-realization.

Fromm's work provides many insights about the age-old question of cultural influences versus invariant aspects of human beings. Fromm focuses on both, which has helped me think about their interplay in myself and others. The invariants, the aspects of us that are "simply human," include needs such as the needs for relatedness, a sense of identity, transcendence, a frame of orientation, and an object of devotion (Funk, 2019).

At the same time, each of us is a product of a particular culture and era. My own early writing focused on universality as well as cultural and individual differences in emotional experience and expression. The work of Carroll Izard (1972, 1977) in the 1970s suggested that each fundamental or discrete emotion shows itself in a characteristic facial expression, with specific muscle movements associated with it. The discrete emotions Izard and I (1978) studied were interest (curiosity), joy, surprise, sadness, disgust, contempt, anger, fear, shame, and guilt. Let me emphasize that these emotions belonged in this category because each had a characteristic facial pattern and other features, and not because they were more significant than, for example, loneliness. While we thought of these emotions as universal, we had no doubt that culture plays a role in *what triggers an emotion and how it is experienced and expressed.* In fact, a very significant mentor of Izard's, Silvan Tomkins (1962, 1963), developed a whole theory about the socialization of emotions, suggesting that each human being is partially a product of what we have been *taught to feel about what we feel.* Cultural, temporal, and individual factors affect this process.

Social Conditions Conducive to Human Growth

In his public addresses and in his books and articles, Fromm passionately promoted ideas about how society could facilitate human growth. For example, in the ringing quote that I often return to:

> No man is a means toward another's ends but always and without exception an end in himself; where nobody is used, nor uses himself, for purposes which are not those of the unfolding of his own human powers; where man is the center, and where all economic and political activities are subordinated to the goal of his growth.
>
> (1955, p. 276)

For Fromm, economic conditions and social mores contribute to the shaping of our conscious minds, so it is imperative that they are conducive to healthy development. Societies differ in how they organize work life and social life. Of primary concern for Fromm is whether or not they are shaped in such a way as to promote the fullest flowering of the individual's capacities.

In *The Heart of Man* (1964), Fromm spells out some of the conditions that facilitate growth, including economic and psychological abundance (versus scarcity), the abolition of injustice (versus exploitation), and freedom (freedom from shackles and freedom to create). Fromm returns to the elucidation of these views in much of his work. By seeing society as pivotal in the development of the individual, Fromm integrated psychoanalytic and sociological ideas in a unique sociopsychological approach (Funk, 2019). At the heart of Fromm's vision of health is his belief in humanism. I discuss Fromm's pivotal conceptions of humanism, socio-humanism, and humanistic alternatives in chapter four on Fromm as a philosopher.

Many influences, including his own experiences of world wars, his orthodox Jewish upbringing, and his intensive sociological, anthropological, psychoanalytic, philosophical, and theological studies led Fromm to his views on society, but the influence of Marx is particularly noteworthy. Fromm studied Marx's writings beginning in 1920 and referred to them throughout his writing career, as a cornerstone of *Marx's Concept of Man* (1961a) but in many other works as well.

A significant chapter of *On Being Human* (2005) is devoted to Marx's contributions. Here, Fromm spells out some of the Marxian concepts that have greatly influenced his own thinking. For example:

> Marx assumed the greed for money to be the *product* of certain social circumstances, not an "instinct" that was the *cause* of these circumstances. His aim was the liberation of man from crippledness, from his loss of himself, from his alienation. The socialist society was not an aim in itself, but a means to the full realization of man.
>
> (p. 133, italics in original)

I discuss Fromm's emphasis on the problem of alienation at greater length in the chapter on contemporary issues, since it is highly pertinent to an understanding of Fromm's relevance to the challenges we face today.

For Fromm (2005), a crucial aspect of Marx's thinking is that the threat of alienation could only be overcome by the creation of a totally new social structure that centers on our being able to enjoy the products of our labor without becoming slaves to them. For Fromm, what was truly revolutionary in Marx was the emphasis on a shift away from alienation and the structural changes in society were to be a *means* to that end and not an end in themselves. *Society needed to change in order for human beings to attain the highest possible development of our capacities for reason and love.* The full realization of our potential is the goal. The purpose of making changes in the structure of society is to facilitate human self-development. As Fromm sees it, Marx's objectives and vision for humankind have been overlooked in favor of focusing on the structural changes Marx advocated. One view of Marx is that he was simply advocating for workers to have a greater share of wealth; for Fromm, that is far from a correct reading. Fromm's view is that Marx was arguing for a change in our orientation from a "having" mode to a "being" mode, a central theme in *To Have or To Be?* (1976).

Fromm roots one of his most memorable statements in Marxian theory. He credits Marx with the thought that it is part of our human nature to express our faculties toward the world, rather than to use the world as a means to satisfy our physiological needs. In Fromm's beautifully expressive words:

> [B]ecause I have eyes I have the need to see; because I have ears I have the need to hear; because I have a brain I have the need to think; and because I have a heart I have the need to feel. In short, because I am a man, I am in need of man and of the world.
>
> (2005, p. 156)

For me, this has always been one of Fromm's key declarations. Personally, I link it to the flavor of the thinking in the Apocrypha that emphasizes the degree to which we *use* our talents, rather than on the *number* of our talents. It has always been extremely meaningful to me, as a clinician and as a person, to hold this value.

In sum, Fromm (2005) sees Marx as a bold, utopian revolutionary who challenged us to think, act, and actually become different. Fromm attempted something similar in his own writing, speaking, teaching, and political activities. McLaughlin's (2021) study of Fromm as a "public sociologist" gives us a balanced view of Fromm's theoretical strengths as well as his weak points. In his conclusion, McLaughlin cites Fromm's relevance in understanding current political trends in the USA: "No single intellectual has a better theoretical response to the despair and anger that is feeding reactionary views than Fromm" (p. 238). Summing up, McLaughlin states:

> "Fromm had his limitations as all political actors and theorists do given our common and flawed humanity. Nonetheless, Fromm's commitment to theoretical ideas and the research tradition he created provides an invaluable set of intellectual resources for global public sociology for the twenty-first century."
>
> (p. 239)

Note

1 Unless otherwise indicated, all biographical information is from Burston (1991), Cortina and Maccoby (1996), and Funk (2000, 2019).

References

Buechler, S. (1988). Joining the psychoanalytic culture. *Contemporary Psychoanalysis*, 24, 462–470.

Burston, D. (1991). *The legacy of Erich Fromm*. Harvard University Press.

Cortina, M. & Maccoby, M. (Eds) (1996). *A prophetic analyst: Erich Fromm's contribution to psychoanalysis*. Jason Aronson.

Frie, R. & Sauvayre, P. (Eds) (2022). *Culture, politics and race in the making of interpersonal psychoanalysis: Breaking boundaries*. Routledge.

Fromm, E. (1941). *Escape from freedom*. Farrar & Rinehart.

Fromm, E. (1947). *Man for himself*. Rinehart.

Fromm, E. (1950). *Psychoanalysis and religion*. Vail-Ballou Press, Inc.

Fromm, E. (1955). *The sane society*. Henry Holt and Company.

Fromm, E. (1956). *The art of loving*. Harper & Row.

Fromm, E. (1961a). *Marx's concept of man*. Frederick Unger Publishing Company.

Fromm, E. (1961b). *May man prevail? An inquiry into the facts and fictions of foreign policy*. Doubleday.

Fromm, E. (1962). *Beyond the chains of illusion: My encounter with Marx and Freud*. Simon & Schuster.

Fromm, E. (1964). *The heart of man: Its genius for good and evil*. Harper & Row.

Fromm, E. (1968). *The revolution of hope*. Harper & Row.

Fromm, E. (1976). *To have or to be?* Harper & Row.

Fromm, E. (2005). Karl Marx. In *On being human* (pp. 132–158). Continuum.

Fromm, E. & Maccoby, M. (1970). *Social character in a Mexican village: A sociopsychoanalytic study*. Prentice-Hall.

Funk, R. (1982). *Erich Fromm: The courage to be human*. Continuum.

Funk, R. (2000). *Erich Fromm: His life and ideas*. Continuum.

Funk, R. (2019). *Life itself is an art: The life and work of Erich Fromm*. Bloomsbury Academic.

Izard, C. E. (1972). *Patterns of emotion*. Academic Press.

Izard, C. E. (1977). *Human emotions*. Plenum Press.

Izard, C. E. & Buechler, S. (1978). *Emotion expression ontogeny and cognitive attainments.* Grant application, received funding by National Science Foundation.

McLaughlin, N. (2021). *Erich Fromm and global public sociology.* Bristol University Press.

Tomkins, S. S. (1962). *Affect, imagery, consciousness, Vol. 1: The positive affects.* Springer.

Tomkins, S. S. (1963). *Affect, imagery, consciousness, Vol. 2: The negative affects.* Springer.

Chapter 3

Fromm the Activist

Fromm argued passionately for psychoanalysts' active involvement in politics. In "In the Name of Life: A Portrait through Dialogue" (1986a), he pleads:

> [I]f we love our fellow humans, we cannot limit our insight and our love only to others as individuals. That will inevitably lead to mistakes. We have to be political people, I would even say passionately involved political people, each of us in the way that best suits our own temperaments, our working lives, and our own capabilities.
>
> (p. 116)

I think each of us must find our own way to rise to Fromm's challenge.[1]

What is so inspiring to me is that Fromm really practiced what he preached. He had no difficulty with embodying both the role of a psychoanalyst and the role of a political activist. He saw those roles as complementary in that, in each, he was expressing the values he articulated in his writing. He lived his values in every aspect of his professional life. That, itself, expresses his belief in love as an *activity*, regardless of whether it is love for a particular person or for all human beings. Fromm embodied his love for humanity in his fervent political actions.

I also draw inspiration from *how* Fromm fought for his beliefs. He used his strengths as a persuasive writer to fight for the causes he cared about. Both his words and his example persuaded me to

DOI: 10.4324/9781032693521-6

think about the place of integrity in the work and life of a clinician. The concepts of integrity, wholeness, and consistency between word and action formed the basis of a chapter of my first book (Buechler, 2004), but it also plays an important role in many of my papers and other books as well as in my own clinical work and personal life.

In my psychoanalytic training at the William Alanson White Institute in New York, Fromm's influence was sometimes palpable. I heard "echoes" of his passions in many of my supervisors and in my personal analyst. The chapter in the present volume on inspiring beginning clinicians expresses these "echoes" in some detail.

Embodying values in political action can have a powerful impact. Fromm left us many examples of this. While the expression of his political fervor took many forms, I will concentrate on four activities. Of course, as an author of many books dealing with cultural, societal, political, and psychological issues, Fromm had political impact, but I describe this aspect of his career in a separate chapter on his work as an author. For clarity, I have grouped Fromm's expressly political activities on the world stage into four categories, although, of course, these efforts overlapped.

Activities on Behalf of Humanistically Oriented Governmental Policies

Fromm's book *May Man Prevail?* (1961b) examined the Cold War and argued in favor of ending it. In 1960, speaking at various universities in the US, he lectured about the Socialist Party, gathering overflowing crowds. He reached out to many Socialist Party members, including Norman Thomas. Fromm championed what he called *humanist socialism*, which was based on the work of Karl Marx, with an emphasis on the promotion of self-expression and self-realization. Fromm fought to have some impact on political decision making in the US, and he approached this goal by using his gifts as a writer and speaker to try to convince others to become allies. His belief was that only through this philosophy could we avoid catastrophe.

Fromm spelled out his version of the humanistic (as opposed to the purely economic) values of socialism in "Humanist Socialism" (1960). Here, he states:

> "The supreme principle of socialism is that man takes precedence over things, life over property, and hence, work over capital; that power follows creation, and not possession; that man must not be governed by circumstances, but circumstances must be governed by man."
>
> (p. 66)

Further in this essay, Fromm declares that no one should be made into a means to another's ends. This perspective is based on each of us being connected through our shared humanity. Thus, it is necessary for us to be loyal to the human race, rather than worshipping the State or any one nation or class. Fromm's humanistic socialism is opposed to war, armament, and any effort to solve political and social problems through violence. Fundamentally, Fromm was searching for a way that basic necessities would be accessible for all, human creativity would be nurtured, and political and economic freedom achieved. Fromm's humanistic socialism also stands for religious freedom and the separation of church and state. His lofty goals were spelled out, as well as some suggestions for their implementation, in this essay. These principles led Fromm to support the American Socialist Party. Fromm hoped that this party could fashion a socialism that fulfilled twentieth century needs. He believed that, while the details of realizing these aims were formidable, they were as achievable as the goals in other fields, such as the natural sciences. At the end of the essay, Fromm writes this passionate plea:

> We appeal to every citizen to feel his responsibility for his life, that of his children, and that of the whole human family. Man is on the verge of the most crucial choice he has ever made: whether to use his skill and brain to create a world which can be, if not a paradise, at least a place for the fullest realization of man's potentialities, a world of joy and

creativity—or a world which will destroy itself either with atomic bombs or through boredom and emptiness.

(1960, p. 88)

In contrast with some of the critical characterizations of socialism, Fromm declares that, at least in the form he favors:

"Socialism is not only a socioeconomic and political program; it is a human program: the realization of the ideals of humanism under the conditions of an industrial society. *Socialism must be radical. To be radical is to go to the roots; and the root is Man.*"

(p. 89, italics in original)

Funk (2000) quotes from a letter Fromm wrote in 1962 to Adam Schaff, a Polish Socialist:

"I have been a socialist since my student days forty years ago but have never been active politically until the last five years, when I have been very active in helping to form an American peace movement, on the left-wing of which I find myself."

(p. 148)

It is these principles that led Fromm to speak and write in support of American socialism. In 1960, Fromm formally joined the American Socialist Party and wrote their party platform for that year (Burston, 1991). He traveled to various parts of Europe during the 1960s promoting Socialist ideals. Fromm believed that many had distorted and dismissed Marx's writing and sought to correct the record in *Marx's Concept of Man* (1961a). In many talks, books, and papers, Fromm emphasized the early work of Marx, with its focus on human growth. McLaughlin (2021) writes that Fromm was a popular speaker on college campuses in the 1960s and drew many new recruits to his version of socialism.

Fromm was acutely aware of the dangers facing the US and the wider world. He worked in various ways to promote humanistic values in the conduct of politics. Here are his political goals, in his own words, from the last pages of *The Heart of Man* (1964):

[T]here is idolatry of national sovereignty, a lack of objectivity and reason in foreign policy. On the other hand, there is the wish, among the majority of the populations in both blocs, to avoid the catastrophe of nuclear destruction; there is the voice of the rest of mankind, which insists that the big powers should not involve all others in their madness...

(p. 141)

Indeed, we must become aware in order to choose the good—but no awareness will help us if we have lost the capacity to be moved by the distress of another human being, by the friendly gaze of another person, by the song of a bird, by the greenness of grass. If man becomes indifferent to life there is no longer any hope that he can choose the good. Then, indeed, his heart will have so hardened that his "life" will be ended. If this should happen to the entire human race or to its most powerful members, then the life of mankind may be extinguished at the very moment of its greatest promise.

(p. 150)

For Fromm, it was most important to work toward moving the country in the right direction. In "Is Man Alive?" (1968), he "diagnosed" the severity of our political state, and the significance of getting the country on a healthier track:

I would compare us with a patient on the critical list. In other words, there is the possibility, and if I let only my thinking speak, perhaps even the probability that we are headed for the megamachine or for the technotronic society, and for the extinction of individuality, and that means for culture as we have known it. But I also believe there is a great probability that we're headed for thermonuclear war. But I think all this is not a necessity. That there is so much in a protest longing for life, awareness of what's going on, that there is a possibility to change our course. And what I mean is, it doesn't matter so much whether we go 10 miles or 100 miles in another direction; what really matters is whether we change

the direction. The faster one goes in the wrong direction the
faster one gets into catastrophe.

(p. 7)

McLaughlin (2021) chronicles Fromm's eventual disappointment
with socialism. While Fromm was effective in bringing new
recruits into the party, he was unable to sway the party toward his
platform: "Legitimate political critiques of communist tyranny
led some progressive activists to support fanatical anti-commun-
ism which in turn led them to right-wing, albeit pro-labor, politics" (pp. 161–162). By the time Fromm was living in Switzerland,
he had become disillusioned. McLaughlin suggests that Fromm's
temperament and overcommitment to too many responsibilities
ultimately limited his impact on the party.

As I read it, some of Fromm's greatest assets also had a price
(as, I believe, is often true). On the one hand, Fromm's outsider
position in several fields enabled him to be a great critic, his
multidisciplinary, multinational, multi-issue approach contributed
to his insight, and his ambitious goals added to his reach. But,
inevitably, they also resulted in a less concentrated focus on the
details of how to realize his vision for the socialist party.

Anti-Vietnam War and Work toward World Peace

Fromm's well thought out pleas, first written in 1966 as a letter to
the Pope to convene a world conference on behalf of peace, were
published in *On Being Human* (Fromm, 2005) along with other
material from his "memos."

Fromm's dream for society was reflected in what he called the
"messianic idea" of the prophets (Fromm, 1986b):

It was to establish a new peace that was more than just the
absence of war; it was to establish a state of solidarity and
harmony among individuals, among nations, between the
sexes, between man and nature, a state in which, as the prophets say, man is not taught to be afraid...In their eyes, that
would be a time of abundance-not of luxury, but of abundance in the sense that for the first time the table would be set

for everyone who wanted to eat at it, for everyone who, as a human being, had the right to sit at that table and join in the shared meal with all other human beings.

(pp. 137–138)

McLaughlin (2021) writes of the personal background that contributed to Fromm's involvement in the politics of human rights. Fromm worked to free his cousin, Heinz Brandt, from an East German prison, where he was incarcerated for his political beliefs. This spurred on Fromm's involvement in the organization Amnesty International, which took a position against political persecution. In McLaughlin's words, "Fromm knew, as some academic Marxists do not, how authoritarian Stalinist Marxists could be" (p. 154). Personal experience informed his human rights activism, as well as his financial support of Amnesty International.

Establishment of SANE and Other Anti-Nuclear Activism

Fromm co-founded SANE (the National Committee for a Sane Nuclear Policy) in 1957. According to McLaughlin (2021), Fromm's attendance at a Bear Mountain Lodge peace meeting played an important role in furthering his anti-war and anti-nuclear activism. On October 1, 1960, Fromm spoke at a SANE rally in Boston. He was passionately committed to fighting against the arms race, the dangers of nuclear armaments, and the tragedy of war. McLaughlin calls Fromm SANE's most famous and visible speaker and writer. In 1962, along with Homer A. Jack, Fromm represented the American peace movement at a congress in Moscow. Fromm spoke about the reasons disarmament efforts failed and his opposition to nuclear armament in West Germany.

In a fundamental sense, Fromm saw it as a responsibility to oppose the spread of nuclear weaponry. His essay, "Disobedience as a Psychological and Moral Problem" (1963), memorably declares that "...human history began with an act of disobedience, and it is not unlikely that it will be terminated by an act of obedience" (p. 1). With this statement, Fromm suggests that the story of Adam and Eve and the story of Prometheus represent acts of disobedience that were necessary in order for humankind to become fully human. However:

> "If mankind commits suicide, it will be because people will obey those who command them to push the deadly buttons; because they will obey the archaic passions of fear, hate, and greed, because they will obey the obsolete cliches of State sovereignty and national honor."
>
> (p. 4)

With striking clarity and passion, Fromm (1967) declares:

> The existence of the entire human race is threatened by the madness of preparing nuclear war. Stone age mentality and blindness have led to the point where the human race seems to be moving rapidly toward the tragic end of its history at the very moment when it is near to its greatest achievement.
>
> (p. 18)

Fromm frames it as a duty to speak out against this outcome.

Sadly, Fromm became extremely troubled about the likelihood of atomic war. In 1962, in a letter to the British writer Clara Urquhart, Fromm wrote:

> The other night I wrote a kind of appeal which is centered around the love of life. It was born out of a mood of despair which made me feel that there is hardly any chance that atomic war will be avoided, and sudden insight in which I felt that the reason why people are so passive toward the dangers of war lies in the fact that the majority just don't love life. I thought that to appeal to their love of peace or to their fear of war might have more impact.
>
> (Funk, 2000, p. 150)

For me, this statement is both poignant and emblematic of Fromm's sophisticated viewpoint about human motivations. Like the emotion theories with which I am most familiar (Izard, 1972, 1977; Buechler, 2008), Fromm bases his thinking on a *balance* of emotion-based motives. If the passion for life is not strong enough, it will not hold sway. Much of Fromm's career was dedicated to the idea that it must prevail over all other forces.

Efforts on Behalf of the Campaign of Eugene McCarthy for President of the US

Fromm took an active role in the campaign, including "ghost-writing" speeches for the presidential bid of Eugene McCarthy. He traveled all across the country, speaking and arranging events to promote McCarthy's candidacy. One sentence from the 1968 speech he wrote for McCarthy stands out for me: "We need reconciliation within ourselves-between the values that we profess and the values that motivate us in our daily life" (Fromm, 2005, p. 89). Fromm goes on to name some of our professed values, like reverence for life, love and compassion, reason, brotherhood, and faith in the human potential to grow. But, he continues, we do not live our political and personal lives according to these values. For example, in Vietnam we:

> "conduct a war against a small nation, destroying human beings day after day, because we have made it part of our political creed that we must save the freedom of these people, even if we destroy them in the process."
>
> (p. 89)

Striking to me, aside from the bluntness of speech and the passion behind the words, is Fromm's argument that we need to stop the war in Vietnam to save *ourselves*. That is, we cannot achieve reconciliation within ourselves unless our actions reflect our stated values. Fromm's *effortfulness* for the causes he embraced, the *content* of his political statements, his clinical *behavior*, and his psychoanalytic theoretical *position* all ring with messages in tune with his stated values. They form a coherent whole.

Note

1   Unless otherwise indicated, the biographical data in this chapter is from Burston (1991), Cortina and Maccoby (1996), and Funk (2000, 2019).

References

Buechler, S. (2004). *Clinical values: Emotions that guide psychoanalytic treatment*. The Analytic Press.

Buechler, S. (2008). *Making a difference in patients' lives: Emotional experience in the therapeutic setting*. Routledge.

Burston, D. (1991). *The legacy of Erich Fromm*. Harvard University Press.

Cortina, M. & Maccoby, M. (Eds) (1996). *A prophetic analyst: Erich Fromm's contribution to psychoanalysis*. Jason Aronson.

Fromm, E. (1960). Humanist socialism. In *On disobedience* (pp. 65–89). Harper Perennial.

Fromm, E. (1961a). *Marx's concept of man*. Frederick Unger Publishing Company.

Fromm, E. (1961b). *May man prevail? An inquiry into the facts and fictions of foreign policy*. Doubleday.

Fromm, E. (1963). Disobedience as a psychological and moral problem. In *On disobedience* (pp. 1–13). Harper Perennial.

Fromm, E. (1964). *The heart of man: Its genius for good and evil*. Harper & Row.

Fromm, E. (1967). Prophets and priests. In *On disobedience* (pp. 13–39). Harper Perennial.

Fromm, E. (1968). Is man alive? Interview with Edwin Newman. *Fromm Forum*, 16, 1–13.

Fromm, E. (1986a). In the name of life: A portrait through dialogue. In *For the love of life* (pp. 88–117). The Free Press.

Fromm, E. (1986b). The relevance of prophets for us today. In *For the love of life* (pp. 134–140). The Free Press.

Fromm, E. (2005). Campaign for Eugene McCarthy. In *On being human* (pp. 88–96). Continuum.

Funk, R. (2000). *Erich Fromm: His life and ideas*. Continuum.

Funk, R. (2019). *Life itself is an art: The life and work of Erich Fromm*. Bloomsbury Academic.

Izard, C. E. (1972). *Patterns of emotion*. Academic Press.

Izard, C. E. (1977). *Human emotions*. Plenum Press.

McLaughlin, N. (2021). *Erich Fromm and global public sociology*. Bristol University Press.

Chapter 4

Fromm the Philosopher

What Is Universally True About Being Human?

> Making the unconscious conscious transforms the mere idea of the
> universality of man into the living experience of this universality; it is
> the experiential realization of humanity. To experience my uncon-
> scious means that I know myself as a human being, that I know that
> I carry within myself all that is human, that nothing human is alien
> to me, that I know and love the stranger because I have ceased to be
> a stranger to myself. The experience of my unconscious is the
> experience of my humanity, which makes it possible for me to say to
> every human being, "I am thou." I can understand you in all your
> basic qualities, in your goodness and in your evilness, and even in
> your craziness, precisely because all this is in me, too.
>
> (Fromm, 1963, p. 7)

The idea that there is an essence of being human has been
expressed and debated in many contexts, including philosophical,
sociological, psychological, and religious writing. It is a cornerstone of my own thinking, throughout my career. In my first book
(Buechler, 2004), I examined values—curiosity, kindness, courage,
integrity, and emotional balance—that I consider to be at the
essence of both the therapeutic endeavor and, more generally,
the human condition. In my second book (Buechler, 2008), I
wrote about "fundamental emotions"—joy, sadness, anger, shame,
and fear—that I assume to be part of life, regardless of the era or
culture in which we are born. In my subsequent work (Buechler,
2015, 2017, 2019), I described some characteristic human coping

DOI: 10.4324/9781032693521-7

patterns that are present in both clinicians and their patients. All of these books and papers rest on the idea that there are commonalities across human beings. In a sense, were it not for these similarities, it would be hard to imagine the empathic process that allows us to understand other people. While each of us has a particular history and our own version of the phases of life, there is enough overlap to help clinicians "get" what their patients describe. Poets, too, rely on commonalities, assuming their readers have life experience that, for example, demonstrates the sorrow of a love lost forever.

I come to the subject of human commonalities from studying it in Shakespeare's plays. More than anyone else I have read, Shakespeare understood what it feels like to truly love for the first time (*Romeo and Juliet*, 2012), to doubt whether to be or not to be (*Hamlet*, 2016), and to lose the one person who has come to mean more than anything else in the world (*King Lear*, 1997).

Hamlet knows that the best way to reach an audience is to confront them with emotions we all feel, at one time or another. He tells the actors "…to hold as 'twere / the mirror up to Nature to show Virtue her feature, / Scorn her own image" (Act III, scene 2, lines 21–23). Fromm, who I think of as our most Shakespearean analyst, also knew that nothing human was alien to him. He translated that into precepts for clinicians (see Chapter 5). He also hoped to create an institute for the study of human experience. We learn from Rainer Funk (2010) that this hope failed to come to fruition. But I think we can learn much from his plans for the institute's aim, which was "…to pursue the scientific study of man in the spirit of humanism" (Fromm, 2010, p. 103). The institute's basic premise would be that "…in spite of all differences man is one species, not only biologically and physiologically but also mentally and psychologically" (p. 103).

The next sections spell out more of Fromm's philosophical position and how it has informed my own thinking.

Humanism

According to Rainer Funk (2010), over time, Fromm became more skeptical about whether society could overcome forces against life. His belief was that the only hope would be for highly competent thinkers to put their energies into forging a science of man, placing the study of the human being at its center. As already mentioned above, for a time Fromm hoped to create an institute with this mission, but it never came to pass.

However, Fromm's writing makes frequent reference to the concept of humanism as it has been understood in the fields of sociology, philosophy, theology, and psychology, and as Fromm, himself, employed the term. Daniel Burston, who has written extensively about existentialism, humanism, human dignity, and the legacy of Erich Fromm, suggests that humanism is not a singular philosophy or movement but, rather, an outlook. Burston's (2014) summary of the concept emphasizes the unity of the human species, the singularity and worth of every human being, our duty to promote human dignity, our capacity for self-determination, and the significance of actively pursuing freedom.

Fromm frequently referred to humanism. Here are a few ways he described the humanistic subject matter in the institute that he hoped to promote:

> [T]he study of man must be based on certain humane concerns, primarily those which have been the concern of the whole humanistic religious and philosophical tradition: the idea of the dignity of man and of his potentialities for love and reason, which can be actualized under favorable circumstances. Secondly, the study of man must be based on those concerns which result from our own historical situation: the breakdown of our traditional value system, the uncontrolled and unstructured growth of purely intellectual and technical activities, and the resulting need to find a new, rational foundation for the establishment of the values of the humanistic tradition...A humanistic science of man must continue the work of great students of man of the past, such as Aristotle and Spinoza...It is often said by social scientists that one condition of scientific enquiry is the absence of any self-interested or preconceived aims. That this is a naïve assumption is clearly shown by the development of the natural sciences: they are to a large extent furthered and not hindered

by practical aims and necessities. It is the task of the scientist to keep the data objective, not to study without aims—which are what give meaning and impulse to his work. Just as every age has its specific economic and technical problems, so it also has its specific human problems, and the study of mankind today must be prompted and guided by the problems engendered in this period of world history.

(2010, pp. 103–108)

Fromm goes on to name some specific areas of exploration intrinsic to humanistic inquiry: the study of human nature, values, destructiveness, creativeness, authority, the psychological premises of democratic organization, educational processes, and an inclusive history of all of humanity.

Personally, I am drawn to Fromm's humanistic goals. I especially appreciate his point that scientific study must have motivating aims. It is the *data itself* that must be objective. I appreciate that this is difficult to achieve. But, without this distinction, how can we pursue any research founded on humanistic principles? For me, Fromm's point parallels my own struggle with the concept of neutrality in treatment (see Chapter 5). The challenge of the humanistic theoretician, like the challenge of the humanistic clinician, is to draw strength, purpose, and determination from strongly held values, recognize and reveal the perceptual biases they may engender, and strive to see others as they are. Can we see without imposing our own particular social filter? No. But humanistic studies, like psychoanalysis, are best off naming rather than trying to eradicate our biases or, worse still, pretending they do not exist.

The Dangers of Relativism

Part of Fromm's contribution was to focus *both* on human universals and more specific, particular cultural influences. In his concept of the social filter (see Chapter 2), Fromm carefully attended to the influence of society. In fact, his thinking on this subject was a key premise in his overall approach. Fromm's plea was for recognizing *both* the universally human *and* each society's specific impact. Fromm did not sacrifice one in order to focus on the other.

This has led me to try to come up with my own ways to express how we are *simultaneously* products of our common human experience and our particular history. As I will elaborate in the chapter on treatment, I ask new patients to "tell me about the situation you were born into." This is as much a statement as a question. As human beings, we are all born dependent on others for life-sustaining care. But much about child rearing differs according to the culture. My first question in treatment asserts that we have a situation in common: We are all born dependent on an environment we did not create. But, partially shaped by a specific culture, era, and personal history, we all journey from birth to death. Some of life's dilemmas are universal (Buechler, 2019), but the circumstances in which we meet them vary.

Theoretically, the bias inherent in any perceptual process has led some to question whether there can be any objective truth about human nature, a patient's functioning, appropriate goals for their treatment, or many other questions. I take up these issues in the chapters devoted to clinical treatment. There, and in the chapter on Fromm's contemporary relevance, I express my view of the losses we incur if we give up the notion of objective truths, in treatment and more generally as human beings. Here I just mention the difficult task of recognizing our subjectivity without denying essential truths about the human condition. Focusing exclusively on universalities would neglect our significant cultural and societal differences. But if we do not pay attention to our commonalities, we lose the force of Fromm's fervent humanism, a central pillar of his philosophy (Fromm, 1964). To me, honoring Fromm's legacy requires adopting his "binocular" view of the universally human and the culturally specific.

Existential Needs

It is no surprise that Interpersonal analysts in general, including Harry Stack Sullivan and Erich Fromm, focused on our need for human contact and the pain of loneliness when it is unsatisfied.

In 1959, Erich Fromm gave a lecture at the William Alanson White Institute. Rainer Funk (2019) quotes Fromm as having said that, for a human being, whatever his troubles are, the feeling of isolation, whether he is aware of it or not, is the very crux of his suffering.

I am reminded of a poignant scene in *King Lear*, in which the banished, innocent Edgar, seeing the misery of the old king, says, "Who alone suffers, suffers most I'the mind. / Leaving free things and happy shows behind; / But then the mind much sufferance doth o'erskip, / When grief hath mates, and bearing fellowship" (Act III, scene 6, lines 102–105). More than 450 years ago, Shakespeare well understood lonely suffering.

In juxtaposing Fromm's words about the loneliness at the heart of suffering with Shakespeare's similar expression, I am again suggesting that some insights are for all time. They span eras and geography. They are human. In Sullivan's (1953) words, they are more human than otherwise.

Loneliness as the crux of much suffering can be seen as a logical outcome of an Interpersonal viewpoint. Frieda Fromm-Reichmann (1959) emphasized the lack of hope of connection in severe loneliness. Sullivan's (1953) famous, if awkward, statement says, "I, in common apparently with all denizens of the English-speaking world, feel inadequate to communicate a really clear impression of the experience of loneliness in its quintessential force" (pp. 260–261).

Elsewhere (Buechler, 1998, 2012, 2017), I have commented on the analyst's experience of loneliness, so I will not repeat that material. Suffice it to say that it can be the "crux" of suffering on both sides of the couch.

Numerous articles and books have noted the paradox that loneliness is epidemic in our tech connected world (e.g., Leland, 2022). I would suggest that, while loneliness is not new, it may take on different features depending on the cultural surround. In *Seek You*, a graphic portrait of loneliness, Radke (2021) suggests that loneliness is a condition that goes in and out of remission until we die. She quotes two psychiatrists (Jacqueline Olds and Richard S. Schwartz), who suggest that loneliness is a biologically determined, extreme fear of detachment. Poets, psychoanalysts, columnists, psychiatrists, and cultural commentators struggle to find words for the exquisitely human misery of loneliness. We need relationships and suffer without them. This topic receives more attention in the chapter on contemporary issues. In brief, in our vulnerability to loneliness, we are all more human than otherwise.

Expanding this point, Fromm wrote of a number of "existential needs." Rainer Funk (2019) put it this way:

> Because they rank as an existential necessity for human beings, Fromm referred to them as "existential needs." According to Fromm, these include the need for relatedness, the need for rootedness, the need for a sense of identity, the need for transcendence, and the need for a frame of orientation and an object of devotion. These needs must always be satisfied, by each human being in every culture.
>
> (p. 73)

Here are some other statements, by Fromm, of our most fundamental needs as human beings: "Without love, humanity could not exist for a day" (1956, p. 17). For Fromm, we cannot truly love another person without loving all of humanity:

> "If I truly love one person, I love all persons, I love the world, I love life. If I can say to somebody else, 'I love you,' I must be able to say, 'I love in you everybody, I love through you the world, I love in you also myself.'"
>
> (p. 42)

I believe that the well-equipped clinician must be capable of love, in this sense.

> [T]here are also certain psychological qualities inherent in man that need to be satisfied and that result in certain reactions if they are frustrated. What are these qualities? The most important seems to be the tendency to grow, to develop and realize potentialities which man has developed in the course of history—as, for instance, the faculty of creative and

critical thinking and of having differentiated emotional and
sensuous experiences.

(1941, p. 5)

Good and Evil

In the chapter on the clinical Erich Fromm, I discuss conceptions of
good and evil as they influence treatment. Here, I just mention their
impact on how we understand what it means to live a human life.

Questions of good versus evil have preoccupied philosophers,
theologians, and countless others for centuries. In *On Being Human*
(2005a), Fromm distinguishes between the issue as it was framed in
the past and more contemporary versions of it. Briefly, in the past,
evil described *human* motivations, however problematic they were.
But in contemporary culture, as Fromm experienced it, a new form
of evil has arisen. This evil is expressed in the form of profound
alienation. In Fromm's stark appraisal of the phenomenon: "This
attitude of the dehumanized human—of the person who does not
care, of the person who not only is not his brother's keeper but is
not even his *own* keeper—this attitude characterizes modern man"
(p. 29, italics in original). Fromm is describing what he sees as a
pathological but extremely common *indifference*. Fromm understands this as the consequence of our transferring our own human
powers onto our technological creations. In his words:

> We, living people who want to live, are becoming powerless,
> although we are, seemingly, omnipotent humans. We believe
> that we control, yet we are being controlled—not by a
> tyrant, but by things, by circumstances. We have become
> humans without will or aim. We talk of progress and of the
> future, although in reality no one knows where he is going,
> and no one says where things are going to, and no one has a
> goal.

(p. 27)

In part, Fromm is referring to the dangers of atomic weapons,
but one can wonder what he would say about the power over us
of the more sophisticated "things" we have created today.

Indifference as a form of evil is a subject with a long history, in philosophy and elsewhere. Those who experienced severe governmental limitation on life-saving immigration during the Second World War had an especially vivid demonstration of it. Interest in the work of Emmanuel Levinas (Orange, 2010; Severson, 2011) attests to the relevance of the thinking that, as human beings, we have responsibilities toward each other. Severson (2011) writes that habits inherent in culture and history blind us to the ways we reenact past injustices. Even though we cannot possibly answer every current cry for help, we have an obligation to try. Although Severson approaches the topic from a philosophical perspective (and, especially, from his explorations of the philosopher Emmanuel Levinas), I find his emphasis on human obligations consonant with Fromm's thinking about our inter-connectedness.

In a voluminous body of work, Donna Orange (2010, 2016, 2020), a philosopher and psychoanalyst, has explored the ethical dimension in treatment and, more generally, in life. In a ringing testament to Fromm's prescience, after describing how Fromm was excluded from traditional psychoanalytic circles, Orange (2020) declares that the psychoanalytic establishment had silenced:

> a pioneering, interdisciplinary, and creative voice. With Erich Fromm speaking at the IPA and writing in psychoanalytic journals, we might have arrived at the ethical turn decades earlier, challenging the isolation of clinical work from the cultural, social, and ethical/political contexts in which it tries to understand human suffering.
>
> (p. 55)

Influenced by Orange and Fromm, in a personal essay (Buechler, 2021), I explored my own internal experiences of indifference to the suffering of others. I connected my mind's eye's willingness to ignore others' pain with my visual tendency to look away from the poverty, wretchedness, homelessness, and mental anguish evident on the streets of my hometown (New York City) as well as in newspapers and other accounts. I suggested that *visual avoidance may facilitate emotional indifference*. That is, if I am practiced in avoiding staring at the hungry child sitting on my neighborhood sidewalk, I may more easily subsequently turn my mind's *focus* away from newspaper headlines about starvation in various parts of the world. But, in another sense, all indifference may really spring from the same defensive core. I do not want to imagine the gnawing in that homeless, hungry child's belly. I do not want to take the chance that I will then, empathically, feel it in my own belly. Personal and professional experiences have played roles in the development of my defenses, and I have not always been indifferent. But I know I can be or, sometimes, feign being impermeable.

Our limited response (Orange, 2017) to the reality of climate change, with its great threat to the planet, is a constant reminder of our relentless willingness to maintain "business as usual" in more than one sense of the word "business." I believe that we would do well to heed Fromm's pleas that we "wake up" from our alienated state, lest our own creations, our willingness to accede to their impact, and our prioritizing of "business as usual" catastrophically affect the continuance of life itself.

Biophilia and Necrophilia

Fromm's conceptions of biophilia and necrophilia are essential to his understanding of the human condition. In *The Heart of Man* (1964), he spells out these two concepts:

> Literally, "necrophilia" means "love of the dead" (as "biophilia" means "love of life")…The person with the necrophilous orientation is one who is attracted to and fascinated by all that is not alive, all that is dead: corpses, decay, feces, dirt. Necrophiles are those people who love to talk about sickness, about burials, about death. They come to life precisely when they can talk about death.
>
> (p. 39)

The prevailingly necrophilous person lives in the past, nursing memories of what they felt earlier in their lives. They are attracted to the use of force, to law and order. They love the mechanical, inorganic, and are dedicated to having rather than being, to darkness rather than light, and to certainty over uncertainty.

The opposite of necrophilia is biophilia, the love of life. It is an orientation toward preserving life. Biophilia expresses an inherent tendency. This aspect of Fromm's thinking is crucially different from the Freudian perspective about life and death instincts. Whereas Freud understood the human being as innately equipped with both life and death instincts, for Fromm, it is only biophilia that is innate. This has enormous consequences clinically, philosophically, and for those invested in societal change. Briefly, Fromm's theory implies that the presence of *biophilia in an individual needs no explanation since it is an inherent force in human beings, but the presence of necrophilia does.* In my view, nothing could be of greater importance than this concept.

Fromm (1964) sees in biophilia the tendency to preserve life, fight death, integrate and unify, at cellular, emotional, and cognitive levels. Fromm's description of biophilia is so poetic, in my view, that I quote it at length:

> The person who fully loves life is attracted by the process of life and growth in all its spheres. He prefers to construct rather than retain. He is capable of wondering, and he prefers to see something new to the security of finding confirmation of the old. He loves the adventure of living more than he does certainty. His approach to life is functional rather than mechanical. He sees the whole rather than only the parts, structures rather than summations. He wants to mold and to influence by love, reason, by his example; not by force, by cutting things apart, by the bureaucratic manner of administering people as if they were things. He enjoys life and all its manifestations rather than mere excitement. Biophilic ethics have their own principles of good and evil. Good is all that serves life; evil is all that serves death. Good is reverence for life, all that enhances life, growth, unfolding. Evil is all that stifles life, narrows it down, cuts it into pieces.
>
> (p. 47)

Fromm goes on to clearly distinguish his thinking from Freud's view of life and death instincts as both inherent:

> "The death instinct represents *psychopathology* and not, as in Freud's view, a part of *normal biology*. The life instinct thus constitutes the primary potentiality in man, the death instinct a secondary potentiality. The primary potentiality develops if appropriate conditions for life are present…"
>
> (p. 50)

For me, this is one of Fromm's most meaningful statements. Clinically, in my own emotion-centered language, it connects observations of a person's attitudes about surprise, interest, joy in life, love, and other feelings. I discuss biophilia and necrophilia further, in the chapter on contemporary issues. There, I spell out Fromm's ideas about the societal conditions necessary for the biophilic tendency to thrive. Here, I am focusing on biophilia and necrophilia as concepts about the nature of being human, with very different implications from the classical Freudian model. Fromm's thinking is much more complex than may be seen at first. Biophilia and necrophilia are just elements in the multi-factored overall orientations of human beings. They can vary in their constructiveness and destructiveness. In his 1964 book and in other writings, Fromm discusses fundamental questions about freedom and determinism and how substantive change can occur in human beings and in society as a whole. In focusing on Fromm's conceptions of biophilia and necrophilia, I am emphasizing just part of his enormously meaningful philosophy of what matters most in life.

Part of the attraction of Fromm's biophilia/necrophilia conception is that it is inherently hopeful, at least as I read it. If biophilia is an innate tendency that grows under the right conditions, then, at least theoretically, as a society and as individuals, in our relationships we could provide those conditions and promote life. I am in accord with Fromm's linking of openness to the new, willingness to be surprised, and joy. My own language (Buechler, 2004, 2008) describes a dimension of openness to new information (from open-mindedness to closed-mindedness) as reflecting a constantly evolving and relationally influenced process, both within and between individuals. I see a person's emotional state as a system, with changes in the intensity of any emotion as affecting all the others. For me, an innate capacity for joy is the "universal antidote" (Buechler, 2019) to all painful feelings. That is, moments of joy can help us bear life's sorrows, injustices, injuries to our self-esteem, and other hardships. So, basically, I am counting on a positive emotional force to weigh heavily enough in the overall balance. Joy's absence or relative lack of weight is what needs to be explained, since it is assumed to be part of our innate equipment.

Fromm believed that what is important is which trend, biophilia or necrophilia, is stronger since most people have some of each. In a later chapter, I will suggest some of the contemporary versions of necrophilia and the challenges they pose.

Choose Life

Fromm frequently (e.g., 2005b) quoted the Old Testament challenge, "I put before you today Life and Death, Blessing and Curse, and you choose Life" (Deuteronomy 30:19). Fromm's fundamental position, as I understand it, is that we have to live our values, not just recite them. If we love life, we have to show that love in the choices we make. We have the capacity to reconnect with our humanistic roots and save ourselves and our planet from destruction. It is a choice. To make that choice, we have to fully accept that we are part of the whole of humanity, members of one world. When we fully embrace this, we cannot hate the stranger, since the stranger and I are one.

As already suggested in this chapter, this posits the existence of a human essence. Fromm spells this out in *Man for Himself* (1947) and *The Sane Society* (1955). We cannot understand this without accepting the paradox that we are each individuals *and* also what I have (Buechler, 2008) elsewhere referred to as instances of life. We are good and bad, child and adult, criminal and saint (Fromm, 2005b). We are products of a particular time and place and humans with the needs all human beings have had for centuries and will always have in the future. In his "humanistic credo," Fromm (2005c) spells out these essentially human needs. They flow from our awareness of ourselves and our existential situation. We know about being small, in some senses impotent, mortal, and subject to nature's laws. We all must choose between life and death. We invest in a necrophilic, regressive path or a biophilic path forward.

My own work (Buechler, 2004) links these different paths with the extent to which our lives are imbued with a sense of purpose. I focused on the clinician's need to feel our work has abiding purpose, but I believe the need for a sense of purpose exists in us all.

Who Deserves Forgiveness, Empathy, Love?

I see these questions as at the heart (in more than one sense) of much of philosophy and theology. For me, it is Shakespeare who framed the issues, but Fromm also very meaningfully contributed. In his last plays, Shakespeare gives poignant expression to the human need to forgive (e.g., in *The Tempest*, 2011) or, in my language, to "love anyway." The idea of "loving anyway" has informed all my work and my personal life. I think of love as always loving anyway, since there are always reasons not to love someone. And, as my own end draws nearer, I think the ultimate challenge is to love life anyway, that is, to love living despite all the losses, indignities, and suffering it imposes on us, most especially as we age.

Who does not need to love and be loved despite all impediments? The universality of the need to be capable of loving is one of the great truths in Fromm's thinking. He asserts that, in considering the requirements of a healthy life, being able to give love is even more important than being loved. I deal with this in the chapter on the clinical Erich Fromm, where I discuss his views on psychological health.

References

Buechler, S. (1998). The analyst's experience of loneliness. *Contemporary Psychoanalysis*, 34, 91–115.
Buechler, S. (2004). *Clinical values: Emotions that guide psychoanalytic treatment*. The Analytic Press.
Buechler, S. (2008). *Making a difference in patients' lives: Emotional experience in the therapeutic setting*. Routledge.

Buechler, S. (2012). *Still practicing: The heartaches and joys of a clinical career.* Routledge.

Buechler, S. (2015). *Understanding and treating patients in clinical psychoanalysis: Lessons from literature.* Routledge.

Buechler, S. (2017). *Psychoanalytic reflections: Training and practice.* IPBooks.

Buechler, S. (2019). *Psychoanalytic approaches to problems in living: Addressing life's challenges in clinical practice.* Routledge.

Buechler, S. (2021). Empathy with strangers: Personal reflections. *Contemporary Psychoanalysis, 57,* 446–473.

Burston, D. (2014). Humanism. In T. Teo (Ed.), *The encyclopedia of critical psychology* (pp. 915–918). Springer.

Fromm, E. (1941). *Escape from freedom.* Farrar and Rinehart.

Fromm, E. (1947). *Man for himself.* Rinehart.

Fromm, E. (1955). *The sane society.* Rinehart and Winston.

Fromm, E. (1956). *The art of loving.* Harper & Row.

Fromm, E. (1963). *Humanism and psychoanalysis.* Paper presented at the Institute of the Mexican Society of Psychoanalysis, Mexico, DF. March 8, 1963.

Fromm, E. (1964). *The heart of man: Its genius for good and evil.* Harper & Row.

Fromm, E. (2005a). Modern man and the future. In *On being human* (pp. 15–31). Continuum.

Fromm, E. (2005b). The relevance of humanism for today. In *On being human* (pp. 74–83). Continuum.

Fromm, E. (2005c). Some beliefs of man, in man, for man. In *On being human* (pp. 99–105). Continuum.

Fromm, E. (2010). *The pathology of normalcy.* American Mental Health Foundation Books.

Fromm-Reichmann, F. (1959). On loneliness. In D. Ballard (Ed.), *Psychoanalysis and psychotherapy: Selected papers of Frieda Fromm-Reichmann* (pp. 325–336). University of Chicago Press.

Funk, R. (2010). Introduction. In E. Fromm, *The pathology of normalcy* (pp. 9–13). American Mental Health Foundation Books.

Funk, R. (2019). *Life itself is an art: The life and work of Erich Fromm.* Bloomsbury Academic.

Leland, J. (2022). The city has a loneliness problem. *The New York Times,* April 24, pp. 1, 8.

Orange, D. M. (2010). *Thinking for clinicians: Philosophical resources for contemporary psychoanalysis and the humanistic psychotherapies.* Routledge.

Orange, D. M. (2016). *Nourishing the inner life of clinicians and humanitarians: The ethical turn in psychoanalysis.* Routledge.

Orange, D. M. (2017). *Climate crisis, psychoanalysis, and radical ethics.* Routledge.

Orange, D. M. (2020). *Psychoanalysis, history, and radical ethics: Learning to hear.* Routledge.

Radke, K. (2021). *Seek you.* Penguin Random House.

Severson, E. R. (2011). *Scandalous obligation: Rethinking Christian responsibility.* Beacon Hill Press.

Shakespeare, W. (1997). King Lear. In R. A. Foakes (Ed.), *The Arden Shakespeare.* Thomas Learning.

Shakespeare, W. (2011). The tempest. In V. M. Vaughn & A. T. Vaughan (Eds), *The Arden Shakespeare.* Bloomsbury Publishing Company.

Shakespeare, W. (2012). Romeo and Juliet. In R. Weiss (Ed.), *The Arden Shakespeare.* Bloomsbury Publishing Company.

Shakespeare, W. (2016). Hamlet. In A. Thompson & N. Taylor (Eds), *The Arden Shakespeare.* Bloomsbury Publishing Company.

Sullivan, H. S. (1953). *The interpersonal theory of psychiatry.* Norton.

Chapter 5

Fromm the Clinician

Erich Fromm was the teacher of my analyst, my supervisors, and my teachers at the William Alanson White Institute, where I was in training from 1979 until 1983. Everything I have read and heard about Fromm tells me that he had a profound impact on the generation of analysts just before my own.

I first came across Fromm as a college student, and his ideas took greater hold in graduate school and my subsequent career. Ever since I wrote *Clinical Values* (Buechler, 2004), I have been interested in how each analytic theory prepares the clinician for doing treatment. That is, I think that each promotes somewhat different intellectual and emotional strengths.

I was deeply affected by the passionate legacy of Erich Fromm. Fromm clearly saw his role as helping people fight for greater freedom, self-determination, self-actualization, and personal authorship of their lives. For Fromm, living as fully as possible is an achievable and worthwhile goal. He implies that, within us, we all have the power to live freer and healthier lives. In the epigraph to *Escape from Freedom* (1941), he quotes Pico della Mirandola's *Oratio de Hominis Dignitate* as follows:

> Neither heavenly nor earthly, neither mortal nor immortal have we created thee, so that thou mightest be free according to thy own will and honor, to be thy own creator and builder. To thee alone we gave growth and development depending on thy own free will. Thou bearest in thee the germs of a universal life.
>
> (p. vi)

DOI: 10.4324/9781032693521-8

And in the book's last chapter, Fromm declares:

> "The only criterion for the realization of freedom is whether or not the individual actively participates in determining his life and that of society, and this not only by the formal act of voting, but in his daily activity, in his work, and in his relations to others."
>
> (p. 300)

Of course, Fromm gave great importance to societal forces, but he zealously championed the analyst's role in stirring in patients a firm belief in personal agency.

My own clinical work owes tremendous debts to Erich Fromm. I would say he inspires me more than any other writer. His work does not spell out a method or technique for doing treatment, so much as he fires us up to become what he called physicians of the soul. I will try to convey this spirit.

Psychological Health According to Fromm

For Fromm, health is a *relative absence of dissociation*. He generally preferred to use the term dissociation, rather than repression, for what is not conscious. In his paper, "Being Centrally Related to the Patient," Fromm (2009) explains that the repressed refers to what was conscious and now is not. In contrast, the dissociated can refer to what was conscious *and* what was never conscious, because of society's mores or other factors. Thus, it is a more inclusive term, which allowed Fromm's version of the unconscious to include whatever a particular society filters out of members' awareness. The concept of the "social filter" distinguishes Fromm's thinking from other theories.

Another way we might think about health is that it is the satisfaction of our most basic needs. What are the primary needs of a human being? Fromm has provided several answers to this question:

> This desire for interpersonal fusion is the most powerful striving in man. It is the most fundamental passion, it is the

force which keeps the human race together, the clan, the family, the society. The failure to achieve it means insanity or destruction-self-destruction or destruction of others. Without love, humanity could not exist for a day.

(1956, p. 17)

[T]here are also certain psychological qualities inherent in man that need to be satisfied and that result in certain reactions if they are frustrated. What are these qualities? The most important seems to be the tendency to grow, to develop and realize potentialities which man has developed in the course of history-as, for instance, the faculty of creative and critical thinking and of having differentiated emotional and sensuous experiences.

(1941, p. 315)

Man, then, has two vital needs: one, as far as his physiological constitution is concerned, that of physical survival, and one as far as his mental survival is concerned, sanity.

(1969/2013, p. 3)

In much of his work, Fromm (1941, 1950, 1955, 1968) advised human beings, in general, to challenge society's dictates. Fromm believed we should be skeptical about society's influence. In *The Pathology of Normalcy* (2010) and in much of his other work, Fromm distinguished his position from those who see adaptation to society as a measure of health and as a therapeutic goal. This is a highly significant difference.

Some of Fromm's Concepts about Doing Treatment

Privileging Experience in Sessions over Interpretations

Essentially, as I understand Fromm's perspective, we help people by relating to them in a very direct way, so that they feel less isolated, and by avoiding intellectualization. As he described it: "The task of analysis is that the patient *experiences* something and not that he *thinks* more" (2009, p. 34). Fromm believed that we should not withhold what we see out of concern that the patient is not ready to hear it, because that would not fully reach him. In Fromm's words, when you think you see something, you have to "stick your neck out" (p. 36) and say it. My own way to describe this (Buechler, 2004, 2008) has been that the analyst has to have the courage to voice *inconvenient truths*. Training (including one's personal analysis and supervision) should enable us to become radical truth tellers.

My version of Fromm's idea is that it is primarily life experience that changes people, but, ideally, treatment can make more life experience (both within and outside treatment) possible. In other words, it is interpersonal exchanges (including during treatment) rather than abstract interpretations that are the most powerful agents of change. They help people actually live their lives differently.

Another version of the idea of privileging experience is the concept that change precedes insight, rather than that insight precedes change. In this conception, the patient experiments with new ways of functioning, and their experience provides insight into the reasons for their old patterns. For example, a patient who avoided social contact tried inviting neighbors to her home. As she coped with her anxiety in this unfamiliar situation, she became vividly aware of why she had avoided socializing in the past. We are not aware of patterns we have always followed until we try to alter them. Fromm articulated much the same idea in *The Art of Listening* (1994) when he said that "In general much anxiety which is the basis for the development of a symptom becomes visible, becomes open only when the symptom is frustrated" (p. 114).

Fromm (2009) very clearly warned analysts against intellectualizing. My way to express this is that analysts too often waste time helping patients create a theory about themselves at the expense of changing their lives. It is true that (theoretically) one can do both. But I think all too often ideas *about* the patient take precedence over actual experience in the session. Fully inhabiting this belief can have a great impact on the clinician's focus in sessions as well as the content of interventions.

Promising No More Than We Can Deliver

Fromm (2009) is quite explicit about the damages of implicitly or explicitly making promises in treatment that we may not be able to fulfill. Its results can include a permanent state of anxiety in the clinician. In *Still Practicing* (Buechler, 2012), I explore the demoralization that can accumulate over time when the analyst over-promises. I believe that the damage can include a painfully hollow feeling and, perhaps, a projection of one's own resulting sense of impotence onto the field itself, rendering the analyst despairing about the future viability of psychoanalysis. For the individual analyst, the long-term effect can be a form of burnout, which is not unlike depression. For the field as a whole, the effect can be corrosive.

Personally, I like the way Fromm avoided promising more than he knew he could deliver. He believed that analysts cannot guarantee results, but we can offer "central relatedness" (Fromm, 2009). Here is how he described what *is* possible:

> Then I do not think about myself, then my Ego does not stand in my way. But something entirely different happens. There is what I call a central relatedness between me and him. He is not a thing over there which I look at, but he confronts me fully and I confront him fully, and there in fact is not way of escape.

> (p. 18)

Expanding this idea, I (Buechler, 2012, 2017) wrote about the analyst's "non-narcissistic investments" in the patient's well-being. Here is how I described that investment:

> [W]e should be responsive to the needs and feelings of the patient, but we should not have a personal stake in the patient's life-style choices. We should not be narcissistically invested, that is, worried about how the treatment makes us look to ourselves. We shouldn't need a "success" with this patient to prove ourselves as clinicians. So, from a narcissistic point of view, we are neutral and not dependent on any

particular outcome. But, from a human point of view, the outcome cannot be a matter of indifference to us. Passionate engagement in treatment is a genuine investment in life itself.
(2012, p. 17)

While we cannot ensure any specific outcome, we can determine to dedicate ourselves to a genuine encounter, and we can pledge to examine our part in it. We can endeavor to facilitate the patient's creation of a rewarding life. We cannot know whether a particular person should get married or move to Westchester. We should not promise to have answers to these questions. But we can and, I believe, we should promise to engage with the patient in an honest and passionate process that has at its heart caring about the quality of the patient's life experience.

Directly Facing Suffering

Many personal and professional experiences have taught me that suffering is inevitable in life, and must be faced directly, rather than defensively avoided. Fromm's writing, and his influence on my training analyst, supervisors, and teachers, reinforced that lesson. In Fromm's (2009) own words, we "help the patient be unhappy" (p. 51). Fromm declares suffering is "at least a very real feeling, and is a part of life" (p. 51). My reading of Fromm led me (Buechler, 2010) to consider how analysts' attitudes about suffering affect our behavior in treatment and, more specifically, our work with defenses.

Embracing Contradiction and Paradox

It has been invaluable to me to grasp that the contradictory and paradoxical can be true. I have often taken heart from Fromm's (1973) statement:

"To have faith means to dare, to think the unthinkable, yet to act within the limits of the realistically possible; it is the paradox of hope to expect the Messiah every day, yet not to lose heart when he has not come at the appointed hour."
(p. 485)

For me, this suggests that contradictions do not necessarily mean that we should choose one side to be true and the other false. The Messiah has not come at the appointed hour, but that does not mean we should alter our expectations.

Critiques of Neutrality as an Ideal

I have spent much of my treating and writing career puzzling over the question of *how one's passionate beliefs can be integrated into a sufficiently open therapeutic stance.* One of the most difficult papers I ever wrote was titled "Searching for a Passionate Neutrality" (Buechler, 1999). In that paper (and ever since), I have wrestled with what I could and could not accept about analytic neutrality. Briefly, Anna Freud (1936) (and many analysts since then) suggested that the neutral analyst should maintain an even focus on material coming from the patient's id, ego, and superego. Furthermore, countertransference passions should be held in check, analysts should not impose their values, should refrain from "helpfulness," and should follow the unfolding material, with an unhurried posture.

Fromm's position on analytic neutrality is key to his critique of classical Freudian technique. As I understand it, it evolved from the influences of Groddeck, Ferenczi, Sullivan, Thompson, Horney, and Fromm-Reichmann. Central to Fromm's thinking is his belief that we are inherently social. Actual interpersonal experiences shape both the individual's internal structures and interpersonal patterns. Rather than understanding development as the unfolding of a fixed series of libidinal instinctual drives, Fromm and others of the Interpersonal school see human beings as largely a product of significant experiences in relationships with other people. Coupled with this is a sense that patients need the clinician to be attentive and caring, rather than a detached, neutral figure.

As noted above, Fromm's stance relies on the acceptance of the paradoxical nature of so much of life and treatment itself. As succinctly described by Funk (2000), in Fromm's view, analysts both become their patients *and* remain themselves. They must both forget they are the doctors *and* remain aware of it. These paradoxes must be embraced by the analyst in order to engage in the "center to center" relatedness that treatment requires.

Fromm's theoretical position rendered him an appropriate colleague for Sullivan, Thompson, Fromm-Reichmann, and others who gathered to teach at the Washington School of Psychiatry in Washington, DC and the William Alanson White Institute in New York City. This fortunate partnership gave Fromm a clinical base where his ideas were central and, in the journal *Psychiatry*, a fitting venue for his ideas.

Challenging the concept of neutrality was a very significant aspect of my own training and became a central theme in my writing. In a 1999 paper, I summed up where I stood:

> A neutrality I could embrace would have to leave me free to encourage the patient's active efforts to fight depression. It would have to allow me to present enough of a new relational challenge to foster hope. It would have to include a valuing of urgency about not wasting time. And it would have to leave me free to describe the patient's impact on me, so that I can help him understand the differences between his intentions and his effect.
>
> (pp. 225–226)

This position clearly owes a great deal to Fromm. Fromm pleaded with us to choose life, to embrace and not escape our freedom, to awaken to fervent living. He begged us to care about the society we live in and not just our own small circle. He awakened us to the dangers of becoming society's automatons. He pushed us to question materialistic, acquisitive values. He spoke in a language that reached out to millions of college students (including me). He touched our hearts by appealing to our humanistic inclinations. He made demands. He saw who we could become and wanted us to strive for it, for ourselves, for society, and for life. His legacy is precious to me.

My lifelong goal has been to retain Fromm's passionate convictions without sacrificing patients' freedom to explore all their feelings fully. Basically, the aspect of neutrality we must retain is the openness to hearing everything our patients tell us, verbally and nonverbally, consciously and unconsciously. The conundrum is that we have a duty to promote health *and* a duty to provide a neutral space. The challenge each clinician faces is maintaining a personally resonant tension between these goals.

Fromm (1994) provided us with another description of the analyst's role:

> I think in this process the personality of the analyst is very important; namely, whether he is good company and whether he is able to do what a good mountain guide does, who doesn't carry his client up the mountain, but sometimes tells him: "This is a better road," and sometimes even uses his hand to give him a little push, but that is all he can do.
>
> (pp. 37–38)

To me, this means that, as "mountain guides," we have some ideas about the destination (notions of health) and prior experience getting there with other patients. But we cannot carry the patient; they must actively climb for themselves. Fromm stressed the need for the patient's active involvement in the work. In his own words: "If I were to put anything on the wall of my office, I would put a statement which says: BEING HERE IS NOT ENOUGH" (p. 34). In my own mind, I have integrated Fromm's ideas with something Edgar Levenson (one of my teachers) often reiterated: that a map is not the territory. I take that to mean that, while the "mountain guide" has "maps" of health, only a determined, purposive, energetic, collaborative process successfully traverses the intervening "territory."

In a beautiful essay, Marianne Horney Eckardt (1996) declares:

> We are children of our Western cultural tradition. Our cultural values as well as our personal values are active ingredients in our way of conducting therapy, in what we respond to with pleasure or with concern. We do want to make our patients into beings who are more capable of loving, of being creative and less destructive. Let us affirm the fact that those are our own precious values that guide our enterprises.
>
> (p. 164)

In the chapter in this volume on contemporary issues, I suggest that now, more than ever, as clinicians and as human beings, we need Fromm's conception of fully alive people living collaboratively in a humane society. I hope clinicians can examine how humanistic values can be *integrated* with an open, freeing, non-coercive analytic method. I am aware that this entails grappling with weighty contradictions. But if, as a society, we do not find a way to integrate our values about health into our commerce, our philanthropy, our education, our psychoanalysis, and our daily lives, it could literally cost our lives and the lives of our children and grandchildren.

Other Clinical Implications of Fromm's Stance

Limitations of space require me to merely list some of the clinical implications of Fromm's thinking.

Fromm's (1973) view of aggression prompts me to look for ways it is a response to thwarted needs, such as the need to create a satisfying life. This orients me as I hear the material in the session. It is not unlike the clinical implications of Fromm's thinking for the treatment of depression. Basically, his outlook is that, in order to be healthy, human beings need to actively work toward realizing our capacities. As a clinician, this points me toward looking for ways a suffering person has been unable to fully inhabit their potential.

Fromm's (2010) conception of the "pathology of normalcy" facilitates the analyst's attitude that conforming to society's dictates may not be the healthiest path for some. For example, with patients who present with issues about gender orientation, work satisfaction, and family pressures, Fromm's theory helps the practitioner join the patient in exploring the way of life that will be most fulfilling for that person, rather than automatically assuming that the clinician's role is to foster the patient's adaptation to society's values.

Particularly in the work with patients with a history of abuse, but in all my clinical work, it has been vital for me to believe, along with Fromm, that the truth ultimately sets people free, and that a search for it is a meaningful goal in treatment and the rest of life.

In response to my background in emotion theory and my reading of Fromm, I have developed a clinical approach that highlights the balance between various forces in the patient's motivations (Buechler, 2008, 2019). For example, when confronted with a patient's shame, guilt, sorrow, or other negative feelings, in addition to exploring them, I also wonder what has happened to their curiosity, their hope, their joy.

Joining my background in Sullivan's thinking with my reading of Fromm, I follow the Interpersonal emphasis on relationships within and outside the treatment. I believe that, ultimately, it is life itself that "cures" or changes people, but treatment can make more life experience possible. Sullivan and Fromm are my Apollonian and Dionysian gods. That is, Sullivan's work guided me to approach treatment as occurring in phases (Buechler, 2008, 2012, 2017, 2019), while Fromm's thinking infuses me with passion (Buechler, 1999, 2000, 2004, 2009, 2010). One without the other would be incomplete.

Rather than to look for an unvarying method, I have come to feel that each treatment pair creates their way of working. With some patients, studying their interpersonal history is central; with others, the work with dreams takes center stage. With some, focusing on our relationship is key. The rhythms, activity levels, and focuses of each participant vary from one treatment relationship to another. I think it is in Fromm's spirit to honor this. In fact, Fromm was very explicitly against the idea of a textbook that teaches clinicians an unvarying "psychoanalytic technique." In a foreword to *The Art of Listening*, Rainer Funk (1994) wrote, "The special aspect of his therapeutic method cannot be encompassed in a 'psychoanalytic technique' and the psychoanalyst cannot hide behind the 'know-how' of providing therapy" (p. 9). In another section of *The Art of Listening*, Fromm (1994) outlined the requirements for doing psychoanalytic treatment. Briefly, they include that psychoanalysis is an art, that is, an alive process, not a technique practiced mechanically. Its most fundamental requirement is the analyst's profound concentration. It also requires the analyst's freely working imagination, empathy, and capacity for love (in the sense of reaching toward the patient, being unafraid of losing oneself in the process). Its basic goal is understanding unconscious affects and thoughts. An analyst should answer all questions that are matters of public record and weigh the reasons for answering all else. Fromm ends this discussion with the following recommendation:

> The therapeutic relationship shall not be characterized by an atmosphere of polite conversation and of small talk, but by directness. No lie must be expressed by the psychoanalyst. The analyst must not try to please, nor impress, but rest within himself or herself. That means he or she must have worked on himself or herself.
>
> (pp. 192–193)

The requirement of the analyst's capacity for absolute concentration on the patient was brought home to me in a personal experience. When I was still a candidate, I volunteered to be publicly supervised by Alberta Szalita, MD, one of the senior analysts at my institute. It was an unforgettable experience that has played a significant role in my career. Her concentration on me was palpable. I felt like she saw me profoundly, as though looking through clear water to its depths. It was as though nothing else existed but her and me, even though there was a large audience. I have considered this experience as a benchmark for my own clinical and supervisory work.

As indicated above, I have taken from Fromm the belief that, in treatment, it is usually best to be direct about what I am hearing. So long as the patient has a strong sense that the clinician is operating in their interest, with genuine concern for their well-being, I agree with Fromm that it is usually best to express our observations in direct, succinct language. For example, in explaining the process of treatment, Fromm (1994) tells us "I don't interpret; I don't even use the word interpretation. I say what I hear" (p. 98). Here, Fromm described his way of introducing treatment to a new patient. Basically, he would ask the patient to say whatever came into the patient's mind, and if they were leaving anything out, Fromm asked them to indicate that. As he described his part in the interaction:

> "What you tell me makes me hear certain things, and I tell you what I hear, which is quite different from what you are telling

me or intended to tell me. And then you tell me how you respond to my response. And in this way, we communicate."

(p. 98)

For me, this is as clear a description of my own clinical approach as I could imagine.

I credit Fromm with helping me refrain from "idolatry" toward any particular theory, including his. From very early in my own writing career (Buechler, 1988, 1992, 2004), I thought about psychoanalysis as having a culture, and that each practitioner finds their place in it. Some of us are psychoanalytic "rebels," some more "conformists." How we relate to our professional heritage plays a (usually not conscious) role in every session with patients. As I see it, what is important is our being aware of this. Fromm's views about idolatry, authoritarian control, the price of dissociation, the pull toward escaping freedom, conformism, and adaptation have informed me. In my work, I have explored how these issues play out at various points in a clinical career, from training, through our first professional experiences, later stages, and eventual retirement (Buechler, 2012, 2019, 2023). Fromm's conceptual framework greatly influenced my thinking.

Conclusion: Fromm as an Inspiration for the Clinician

How might we describe the basic equipment of a clinician who is inspired by Fromm's work? I deal with this more fully in the chapter on guiding beginning clinicians, but, briefly, the first quality on my list would be empathic attunement. My thinking about the role of empathy in treatment has evolved a great deal over time. I think it has circled closer to Fromm's. I love what Harold Davis (2009) wrote about Fromm: "His directness was a means of being in touch with a person without physically touching; the essence of empathy" (p. 87).

Fromm stands for a passionate promotion of passion in treatment, which has always directly affected my writing and practice. His privileging of the power of human feeling very much appeals to me. His thinking about hope, his open promotion of biophilia, his distaste for cliché, canned interpretations, and sentiment, his compassionate humanism, his willingness to take positions and stand up for what he believed in, and his championing of freedom have moved me all my adult life.

I take it to be in Fromm's spirit, and in accord with his view of unavoidable complexities, that we hold *both* free exploration and passionate promotion of health as treatment essentials. The best I have been able to do is to see them as points on the opposite ends of a continuum or a kind of mental seesaw. When I veer toward the "passionate" end, I tend to remember the value of neutrality. When I try too hard to occupy neutral territory, I find myself wondering what might be blocking my convictions. For me, this "seesaw" operates similarly to the alternations between an other-directed and an inner-directed focus. That is, for a while I might center on perceptions of the patient's feelings, then find myself moving closer to my own inner experience. Or, momentarily focused on my inner experience, I might then incline toward understanding the patient's. Let me emphasize that this "back and forth" movement *is not* a consciously designed, deliberate "technique," but, rather, a tendency I recognize in retrospect. Clinicians naturally flicker. Our attention wanders from the present to the past, from theory to clinical moment, dream to reality, from other to self, from unwavering principles to open ended curiosities. I think we function best when we are light on our feet.

Erich Fromm challenged us to practice passionately, live courageously, cherish truth, recognize expressions of the life force, face and tolerate insecurity, relate from deep within our centers, promote active hope, embrace life's contradictions, privilege being over having, dream about better lives for ourselves and our patients, stop escaping freedom, become less alienated from our own hidden desires, "other" others less, squarely face life's inevitable suffering, become politically involved citizens, actualize our potential, stay curious, choose life. His inspiration profoundly affects my own strivings, professionally and personally, every day of my life.

References

Buechler, S. (1988). Joining the psychoanalytic culture. *Contemporary Psychoanalysis*, 24, 462–470.

Buechler, S. (1992). Stress in the personal and professional development of a psychoanalyst. *Journal of the American Academy of Psychoanalysis*, 20, 183–191.

Buechler, S. (1999). Searching for a passionate neutrality. *Contemporary Psychoanalysis*, 35, 213–227.

Buechler, S. (2000). Necessary and unnecessary losses: The analyst's mourning. *Contemporary Psychoanalysis*, 36, 77–90.

Buechler, S. (2004). *Clinical values: Emotions that guide psychoanalytic treatment*. The Analytic Press.

Buechler, S. (2008). *Making a difference in patients' lives: Emotional experience in the therapeutic setting*. Routledge.

Buechler, S. (2009). The analyst's search for atonement. *Psychoanalytic Inquiry*, 29, 426–437.

Buechler, S. (2010). No pain, no gain? Suffering and the analysis of defense. *Contemporary Psychoanalysis*, 46, 334–354.

Buechler, S. (2012). *Still practicing: The heartaches and joys of a clinical career*. Routledge.

Buechler, S. (2017). *Psychoanalytic reflections: Training and practice*. IPBooks.

Buechler, S. (2019). *Psychoanalytic approaches to problems in living: Addressing life's challenges in clinical practice*. Routledge.

Buechler, S. (2023). *Shattering illusions of a retired psychoanalyst*. Paper presented at the 19th Annual Meeting of the International Association for Relational Psychoanalysis and Psychotherapy, Valencia, Spain, June 16.

Davis, H. (2009). Directness in therapy. In R. Funk (Ed.), *The clinical Erich Fromm: Personal accounts and papers on therapeutic technique* (pp. 85–88). Rodopi.

Eckardt, M. H. (1996). Fromm's humanistic ethics and the role of the prophet. In M. Cortina & M. Maccoby (Eds), *A prophetic analyst: Erich Fromm's contributions to psychoanalysis* (pp. 151–165). Jason Aronson.

Freud, A. (1936). *The ego and the mechanisms of defense*. Karnac Books.

Fromm, E. (1941). *Escape from freedom*. Farrar and Rinehart.

Fromm, E. (1950). *Psychoanalysis and religion*. Vail-Ballou Press.

Fromm, E. (1955). *The sane society*. Rinehart and Winston.

Fromm, E. (1956). *The art of loving*. Harper & Row.

Fromm, E. (1968). *The revolution of hope*. Harper & Row.

Fromm, E. (1969/2013). My own concept of man. *Fromm Forum*, 17, 1–10.

Fromm, E. (1973). *The anatomy of human destructiveness*. Holt, Rinehart & Winston.

Fromm, E. (1994). *The art of listening.* Continuum.

Fromm, E. (2009). Being centrally related to the patient. In R. Funk (Ed.), *The clinical Erich Fromm: Personal accounts and papers on technique* (pp. 7–39). Rodopi.

Fromm, E. (2010). *The pathology of normalcy.* American Mental Health Foundation Books.

Funk, R. (1994). Foreword. In *The art of listening* (pp. 7–11). Continuum.

Funk, R. (2000). *Erich Fromm: His life and ideas.* Continuum.

Chapter 6

Fromm the Author[1]

By any standard, Erich Fromm was a highly prolific and influential author. In describing his writing routines, Funk (2019) reports that Fromm spent much more time reading than writing. When he was ready to start to write, he usually would put his ideas down, by hand, in one sitting. Then he would read it the next day and might start again if he felt he had not captured what he wanted to express. This might continue until he felt at one with the topic. In other words, Fromm's belief in direct encounter with people also characterized his way of relating to ideas. He would wait to have a manuscript completed until he attained that level of conviction. Funk comments on how Fromm's relationship to writing exemplified his approach to life:

> Because Fromm's writing arose out of a direct and inner encounter with the works of other writers and with a topic, and were not the outgrowth of abstract thought and logical thought processes, many readers feel addressed by them and are able to enter into an inner dialogue with what they read. This once again shows that Fromm neither wanted nor founded a school of thought. Fromm lived and felt what he said and wrote. His own art of living sets an example.
>
> (p. 15)

Fromm's relationship to writing exemplifies his integrity, in more than one sense. It is honest, a truthful rendering of his experience. It is also consonant with his beliefs and values. It expresses the

DOI: 10.4324/9781032693521-9

wholeness, the consistency of word and action, that I think of as a crucial characteristic of the clinician (Buechler, 2004).

What follows is a highly selective annotated list of some of Fromm's books in English. Fromm published an extensive array of papers and other books, aside from those included on this list. His German publications are also not listed here, as well as the many lectures that were not collected in books. This very limited sample is meant to offer the reader my personal experience of the books that have had the greatest impact on my own theoretical and clinical work and my personal life experience. Fromm's cherishing of life, dedication to the betterment of individuals and societies, passionate expression of what most matters, and advocacy for peace, freedom, self-actualization, compassion, and love are reflected in the titles and content of these books. Each transcends categorization. While in the rest of this volume I have tried to separate strands of Fromm's thinking by putting his sociological, philosophical, psychoanalytic, activist, and other ideas in separate chapters, his books really span topics and defy classifications. For example, *The Revolution of Hope* (1968) contains comments relevant to sociology, philosophy, and psychoanalysis and might inspire activists and influence the personal life of the reader. Fromm's transcendence of the limitations of separate fields is an aspect of his prophetic vision. His capacity to integrate insights from several disciplines allows him to penetrate beneath the surface of his own time and reach truths that still apply today.

Escape from Freedom (1941)

Escape from Freedom is a profound study of authoritarianism, the nature of freedom, and the means by which society influences the individual. In this stunningly popular book, Fromm put forward a highly significant concept: the idea of social character. Here is how he defined it: "that part of their character structure that is common to most members of the group. We can call this character the social character" (p. 304); "by adapting himself to social conditions man develops those traits that make him desire to act as he has to act" (p. 311).

The contrast between Fromm's concept of social character and Sullivan's concept of sublimation is extremely interesting to me. Both describe ways that society influences our motives and shapes our behavior. Although Sullivan groups sublimation in the category of defenses, he is clearly describing a necessary piece of our equipment for living. For Sullivan (1956), sublimation is "unwitting substitution of a partial satisfaction with social approval for the pursuit of a direct satisfaction which would be contrary to one's ideals or to the judgment of the social censors and other important people who surround one" (p. 14). Fromm's social character is also an inevitability, but with significant differences. Sullivan is saying that sublimation will not work if it is made conscious. It is as though if we were aware of the bargain we were making, we would not make it. But I think Fromm's message is different. He very much *wants* us to know about the bargains that society has influenced us to make.

In my own language, both sublimation and social character may operate to reduce our obsessive conflicts between what we are supposed to do and what we want to do. The classic expression of this conflict is something like, "I should do my homework, but I want to play baseball. I don't know what to do." I think much energy can go into deciding whether to go to the right or the left, in countless variations of this dilemma. It seems to me that both sublimation and social character give us a way to conform to society's needs without feeling we are sacrificing our own. But I think Fromm worries more about the blind adaptation that can result. Perhaps another way to say this is that Sullivan sees conformity in a more positive light than Fromm does. His work with schizophrenics and others who could not fit into society may play a role in this attitude.

Here is another very significant declaration from Fromm's 1941 book: "We believe that ideals like truth, justice, freedom, although they are frequently mere phrases or rationalizations, can be genuine strivings, and that any analysis which does not deal with these strivings as dynamic factors is fallacious" (p. 322). This important statement counters analytic attitudes that would see such strivings as irrelevant in psychoanalysis or analyze them as unquestionably defensive. It played an important role in my own thinking about the ideals (or, in my language, clinical values) that guide treatment (Buechler, 2004).

Man for Himself (1947)

In the foreword to this book, Fromm states its central idea:

> "[I]n this book I discuss the problem of ethics, of norms and values leading to the realization of man's self and of his potentialities...The value judgements we make determine our actions, and upon their validity rests our mental health and happiness."
>
> (p. v)

Fromm challenges ethical relativism. He openly champions social and individual influences that foster self-development. The stance in this book argues for believing that ethics and psychology are indivisible. Fromm criticizes the relativism that is at least an aspect of classical Freudian psychoanalysis. In contrast, he believes that the study of human nature indicates that "Man's main task in life is to give birth to himself, to become what he potentially is. The most important product of his effort is his own personality" (p. 238). Fromm defines "universal ethics" as having the goal of the unfolding of the human being. He differentiates this concept from "socially immanent" ethics, which are commands and prohibitions designed for the functioning and survival of a particular society.

These ideas promote a conviction that it is possible to describe health and desirable to work toward it in treatment and the rest of life. I see this conviction as potentially contributing to the clinician's sense of purpose. From my point of view, Fromm's courageous stand, articulated in this book, can counter nihilistic, solipsistic, and indifferent attitudes. In the chapter on Fromm's relevance today, I suggest that his views are especially pertinent in our "post truth" era. Relativistic thinking, both within and outside psychoanalysis, has been used to justify blurring lines between true and false, resulting in an "alternative fact" universe. In this and many of his other books, Fromm provided counterbalancing arguments. From my perspective, he also modeled the courage to question our own society's values and stand up for our beliefs.

Psychoanalysis and Religion (1950)

In *Psychoanalysis and Religion*, Fromm contrasts two views of the aim of therapy. The first view, with which he differs, sees treatment as aiming for the patient's better adjustment to society— that is, their greater ability to act like most people in their culture. In contrast, Fromm sides against this perspective and with a second position that holds that our goal should be "optimal development of a person's potentialities and the realization of his individuality" (p. 74).

In subsequent passages in this book, Fromm describes human values, including recognizing the truth, becoming independent and free, human beings as ends in themselves (rather than as the means by which others achieve their ends), relating lovingly, distinguishing good from evil, and listening to the voices of their own consciences. For Fromm, each human being should strive toward the fulfillment of these goals, and clinicians should help their patients in this endeavor. Commentators (Burston, 1991; Funk, 2019) have suggested that this viewpoint was rooted in his studies of societies that supported the rise of Hitler, as well as his more general religious, philosophical, historical, and other research.

In my own work (Buechler, 2019), I have spelled out some of the implications of this way of thinking on the clinician's attitudes toward the fundamental difficulties that face human beings, such as bearing aloneness, mourning, aging, suffering, uncertainty, humiliation, hardship, and helplessness. Cultures attach somewhat different meanings to these issues, but, as I see it, they are recurrent themes. I believe that all clinicians would do well to reflect on our own cultural and individual experiences with these human challenges. For me, Fromm's views in *Psychoanalysis and Religion* (1950) have had major consequences clinically and theoretically. Many patients presented in treatment with difficulties "adjusting" to society's expectations. For some, gender related societal dictates clashed with their identities. Some felt that what society demanded them to do, in order to be seen as "successful," did not align with their desires. It is clear that clinicians who view themselves as adjustment counselors will approach these issues differently from clinicians who see themselves as helping patients listen to their own voices.

My extension of this idea (Buechler, 2019) is that the clinician enacts our own attitude about adaptation in how we relate to psychoanalysis's "rules." I have always (Buechler, 1988) viewed the clinical profession as having a culture, with expectations, rules, outlaws, boundaries, and ways to reward compliance and punish disobedience. We live out our relationship with our professional culture every session. Patients can read so much about our own work-related values from our conduct.

The Forgotten Language: An Introduction to the Understanding of Dreams, Fairytales, and Myths (1951)

This significant text outlines Fromm's approach to the study of dreams and, more generally, symbolic language. Here, Fromm spells out that in dreams we express the whole of who we are and not just the aspect of ourselves our society allows us to know. He also discusses myths and Kafka's novel, *The Trial*.

Fromm strove to make this book accessible to all. He believed "symbolic language is the one foreign language that each of us must learn" (p. 10). I appreciate the spirit of this statement and applaud Fromm's effort to convey his insights in jargon-free prose.

One of the principles beautifully articulated in *The Forgotten Language* is that there are aspects of human experience that are universal:

> Just as we do not need to learn to cry when we are sad or to get red in the face when we are angry, and just as these reactions are not restricted to any particular race or group of people, symbolic language does not have to be learned and is not restricted to any segment of the human race.

(p. 18)

Once again, but in different language from other statements about universality, Fromm puts "flesh" on the "bones" of the idea that we are all "more simply human than otherwise" (Sullivan, 1954). He expresses some ways we are alike in immediately understandable terms. His statement also points to the universality of certain basic emotions, which was the topic of my first research efforts (Izard & Buechler, 1978).

Fromm's approach to dream symbols is consonant with an interpersonal analytic model. Rather than translating symbols into universally applicable, concrete representations (e.g., a cigar represents the penis), Fromm (1951) advises us to look at the context and the life experience of the dreamer: "The particular meaning of the symbol in any given place can only be determined from the whole context in which the symbol appears, and in terms of the predominant experiences of the person using the symbol" (p. 20). For example, for some of us, fire represents a threat, while for others it might conjure up peaceful scenes of sitting by the fireside. Fromm writes of "symbolic dialects" (p. 19) shared by some members of a culture. Elsewhere, my own version of this idea (Buechler, 2008) is that treatment itself is created by each treatment pair. Every analyst and patient have to forge their language, methods, goals, rhythms, and ways of atoning and repairing. While there are universalities, such as the need for a frame and boundaries, there are also "dialects" shared by many patient/analyst pairs and individual variations shaped by their histories of interpersonal experiences. Fromm's approach to dreams, which honors universalities, cultural influences, and individual experiences, can be fruitfully applied to other aspects of the treatment process.

The Sane Society (1955)

Fromm made his conception of healthy integrity in general (and, especially, its manifestation in the workplace) clear in *The Sane Society*. Quoting from C. W. Mills, Fromm uses the 13th- and 14th-century craftsman as an example of a healthy work life:

> "The craftsman is thus able to learn from his work; and to use and develop his capacities and skills in its prosecution.

There is no split of work and play, or work and culture. The craftsman's way of livelihood determines and infuses his entire mode of living."

(p. 178)

In another expression of our need to avoid compartmentalizing, Fromm says, "One cannot separate work activity from political activity, from the use of leisure time and from personal life. If work were to become interesting without the other spheres of life becoming human, no real change would occur" (p. 326).

In Fromm's ideal of a sane society, the worker is encouraged to strive for full self-development and the integration of work into the fabric of one's life as a whole. Elsewhere, I have written (Buechler, 1996) that the ultimate example of compartmentaliza-tion of work and non-work is the Dickensian industrial era sweatshop. In such a setting, most of oneself is irrelevant, forcing the individual to split the "real" self from the "work" self. I suggested that chronic despair is a likely result:

To survive, one would probably become furtive, stealing morsels of pleasure, in secret moments of escape from duty. One would define one's real self, one's real life, as taking place outside work. Thus, there would be two selves—a pas-sive, masked, lifeless work-self, and a pressured, intense "real" self...it is consonant with Fromm's spirit that we keep a watchful eye on the changes in our current work climate, careful of any assumption that so-called progress is always for the good. A team may be no more life-enhancing than a patriarchal employer, if the individual's true voice is still unwelcome. In fact, I wonder if an illusion of team coopera-tion, company concern, and openness to difference might be especially spirit-shattering. The employee must then act as though he can freely speak, hiding wariness in his heart.

(pp. 408, 409)

On another extremely important point, Fromm (1955) differ-entiated his views from Sullivan's. He wrote that "the psychic task which a person can and must set for himself is not to feel secure, but to be able to tolerate insecurity, without panic and fear" (p. 196). This, I think, differs, at least in emphasis, from Sullivan. It has important consequences in technique or, at least, in what is going on in the analyst's mind and in how the analyst understands treatment's methods and goals. In a way, we could say there is a difference in priorities here. Fromm prioritizes the patient becoming able to stand out, to be an individual and realize all that is within. To him, this is more important than avoiding all anxiety. For Sullivan, I think, anxiety avoidance is uppermost.

The Art of Loving (1956)

One of Fromm's many statements about the need for a loving relationship is especially meaningful to me: "I believe that love is the main key to open doors to the growth of man" (2005, p. 101). The need to be loved and to love is certainly prominent in the array of reasons people seek psychological help. In his extremely popular book *The Art of Loving* (1956), Fromm spells out his conception of the *activity* of loving, and its requirements. As he states, "love is an action, the practice of a human power, which can be practiced only in freedom and never as the result of a compulsion" (p. 22). Here, Fromm gets to the heart of the matter (if you will forgive the pun). Loving relatedness is a universal need, different from a compulsion and not about possession but, rather, respectful of the other and preserving the identity of each person. As Fromm (2005) spelled out, "Love is a productive orientation for which it is essential that there be present at the same time: concern, responsibility, and respect for and knowledge of the object of the union" (p. 102).

In one of my books (Buechler, 2019), I focused on the capacity to love and the capacity to be alone as "twins," first conceived in the benign environment of the loving caregiver. Here is how I described this:

> [T]he fortunate person, born into good enough caretaking, will (at some point) become able to withstand impulses to merge or flee in order to feel safe. This well-cared for person

will be able to bear difficult passages of solitude and relationship. The hard moments inherent in both aloneness and connection will not have the power to persuade her that the inner or outer world is unbearably dangerous. In other words, both difficult aloneness and difficult relating will be non-traumatic challenges.

(p. 18)

I suggest that this capacity allows the individual to bear both the difficulties in loving and the challenges of separateness without resorting to either merging or fleeing. I further suggest that, ultimately, being able to love oneself and others facilitates a capacity to love life itself, or what I call "loving life anyway" (p. 19). By this, I mean that each of us must find a way to love life, with all its challenges, sorrows, injustices, and other tribulations.

In other words, building on Fromm's conceptions about love, I formulated my belief that if we are fortunate enough to have had "good enough" parenting, we are more likely to become able to actively love and to bear well periods of aloneness. As has often been the case for me, Fromm's ideas in *The Art of Loving* (1956) formed the basis of my own views.

Quite often, people present in treatment more focused on being loved than on loving. Fromm's view of love as an activity, and, most especially, as an activity that can be cultivated frequently, guided me clinically as well as theoretically. It focused me on what was missing, as well as what was present, in patients' narratives about their lives. An idea like Fromm's definition of active loving can orient clinicians as we listen to a particular person's life story and present circumstances. My own extension of the idea, linking active loving and benign aloneness, sometimes led me to questions that proved fruitful.

One of Fromm's descriptions of love defined it as "the active concern for the life and growth of that which we love" (p. 24). Here, Fromm named a key element of all loving, whether it is love for a child, a partner, a parent, or a friend. Fromm's emphasis on "active concern" enabled me (Buechler, 2008) to think about the love that patients and analysts can have for each other. Fromm's conception opens us to notice many forms of love, including the loving concern expressed by a teacher, mentor, or supervisor, for the life and growth of those we educate. In another statement, he again emphasizes its generative, generous aspect: "Love is an activity, not a passive affect; it is a 'standing in,' not a 'falling for.' In the most general way, the active character of love can be described by stating that love is primarily giving, not receiving" (p. 22).

I think Fromm's view of love has much in common with Sullivan's. For Sullivan (1940), "When the satisfaction or security of another person becomes as significant to one as is one's own satisfaction or security, then the state of love exists" (pp. 42–43). Both Interpersonalists emphasize love's caring aspect.

In this book, Fromm (1956) uses his conception of love to challenge us to care for all humankind:

> "If I truly love one person I love all persons, I love the world, I love life. If I can say to somebody else, 'I love you,' I must be able to say, 'I love in you everybody, I love through you the world, I love in you also myself.'"
>
> (p. 46)

To me, this is a beautiful, enriching perspective. Elsewhere, I have explored (Buechler, 2008) the potential for joy in identifying oneself with all of humanity. Fromm's statement directs us toward that full embrace.

The Revolution of Hope: Toward a Humanized Technology (1968)

> The dynamism of human nature inasmuch as it is human is primarily rooted in this need of man to express his faculties in relation to the world rather than in his need to use the world as a means for the satisfaction of his physiological necessities. This means: because I have eyes, I have the need to see; because I have ears, I have the need to hear; because I have a mind, I have the need to think; and because I have a heart, I have the need to feel. In short, because I am a man, I am in need of man and of the world.
>
> (p. 72)

In the chapter on Fromm as a sociologist, I wrote about how Fromm credited Marx for inspiring this fundamental outlook. It is one of Fromm's most meaningful expressions, from my point of view. It is consonant with the belief, also articulated by Rollo May (1953), that unused potential can precipitate depression. In its declarative language, it champions our need to exercise our faculties and relate to other human beings. For me, it has been an inspiration, particularly in treating depressed patients and in writing about that work. But I think it can apply to everyone.

In *The Revolution of Hope*, Fromm spells out his view of the nature and function of hopefulness in human experience: "To hope means to be ready at every moment for that which is not yet born, and yet not become desperate if there is no birth in our lifetime" (p. 9); "Hope is a psychic commitment to life and growth" (p. 13):

> "Another definition of man would be Homo esperans—the hoping man...to hope is an essential condition of being human. If man has given up all hope, he has entered the gates of hell—whether he knows it or not—and he has left behind him his own humanity."
>
> (p. 60)

Fromm's view of the most significant type of hope is its active form. He credits Ernst Schachtel (1959) with a similar conceptualization.

Hope has been a central topic in much of my own writing. It was the subject of one of my first psychoanalytic publications (Buechler, 1995), and it was the first "clinical value" I wrote about (Buechler, 2004). I certainly recognize Fromm's influence on my view of hope. In a Frommian spirit, I wrote (Buechler, 1995) that I do not believe it is the analyst's hope specifically that engenders hope in the patient, but rather:

> the analyst's whole relationship to life. The patient observes the analyst's struggle to make sense of things, keep going in the face of seemingly insurmountable obstacles, retain humor and courage in situations that seem to inspire neither. The

analyst stumbles, reacts without self-hate, works to recover. The analyst is willing to work hard. She is honest without being crippled by shame. She wants to live even the most difficult moments. She doesn't shrink from what is ugly in herself or the other. She is more interested in growth than in being right, more curious than self-protective. She can be wounded but refuses to be made dead. While in part this attitude may provide a model, and it may be contagious, I think that what mainly creates hope is the patient's experience of finding a way to relate to such a person. For many, this task requires substantive changes, alterations in all components of the emotion system. The deepened curiosity and joy, the lightened envy and hate that results engenders hope.

(pp. 72–73)

The Revolution of Hope also features Fromm's (1968) effort to integrate insights about human potentialities and economic, social, and political realities:

[T]he revolutionary changes necessary to humanize technological society—and this means no less than to save it from physical destruction, dehumanization and madness—must occur in all spheres of life: economic, social, political, and cultural. They must occur simultaneously, since a change in only one part of the system will not lead to the change of the system as such but will only reproduce its pathological symptoms in other forms.

(pp. 155–156)

The Anatomy of Human Destructiveness (1973)

Fromm had a longstanding interest in the roots of human destructiveness. This book is the culmination of years of study. Fromm puts forth the thesis that the primary tendency in human beings is to grow and develop. Destructiveness is generally the result of this tendency being obstructed or blocked in some way. Fromm argues against the idea that destructiveness is primary in human beings. Rather, he says it can be the result of the way a person is living. However, he does also recognize that human beings can have aggressive reactions to threats and fear and calls them "reactive aggression." In making these distinctions, Fromm is differing from Freud's notion of an inherent human "death drive."

Fromm further qualified his thinking on this subject, by adding a character orientation: the "necrophilic," who is attracted to the dead and death itself. But Fromm sees this as an outgrowth of the history of the person, not as an inevitable expression of being human.

Fromm's views of human destructiveness and their bases are open to question, but I, for one, find them extremely helpful as a source of hypotheses in clinical work. With patients, I found it mattered whether I held the belief that aggression is an inborn inevitability, or I considered it as the product of the individual's interpersonal life experience. Fromm's view inclined me to ask different questions and practice with different initial hypotheses than I would have, had I believed in aggression as inevitable.

I also found Fromm's definition of sadism clinically helpful: "I propose that the core of sadism, common to all its manifestations, is the passion to have absolute and unrestricted control over a living being..." (p. 322). Aside from according with my own tendency (as a former emotion theorist) to carefully differentiate motivational states (such as aggression and sadism) that some confuse, I found this way of thinking about sadism helpful in that it pointed me toward looking for the need for control underneath sadistic behavior. For example, with one long-term patient, exploring his history of being humiliated for having dependency needs helped me understand his sadistic, controlling tendencies.

Every theory focuses us differently, in clinical and other situations. To understand aggression as primary, inherent, might incline the patient and clinician to look for ways to inhibit it. This might be useful, and Fromm's thinking does not preclude it. But with his attitude in mind, I think it is more likely we will incline toward looking for developmental and current interpersonal frustrations of the need to grow. Influenced by Fromm, I was better equipped to persist in some treatments. Understanding aggression as innate can lead to a dead end. It can discourage us from feeling there is anything we can do about it. But Fromm's perspective can help us consider how having a more flourishing life could stem the patient's aggression. Clinically, it opens a door to more possibilities and greater hope.

I have often taken heart from Fromm's statement:

> To have faith means to dare, to think the unthinkable, yet to act within the limits of the realistically possible; it is the paradoxical hope to expect the Messiah every day, yet not to lose heart when he has not come at the appointed hour. This hope is not passive, and it is not patient; on the contrary it is impatient and active, looking for every possibility of action within the realm of real possibilities.
>
> (p. 485)

If I had to choose one quotation from Fromm, as a guide for clinical work, I might well choose this one. Aside from its beautiful expression of keeping hope alive, it also crystallizes the paradoxical nature of treatment, and, more generally, of much of life, as I see it.

For the Love of Life (1986)

This is a series of interviews of Fromm in the last decade of his life, edited by Hans Jurgen Schultz and translated from German by Robert and Rita Kimber. There is much wisdom in what I read as a kind of summary of much of Fromm's thinking.

His simple, profoundly humanistic statements get to the heart of what society needs to provide in order for us to flourish. They bring what is good for society and what is good for individuals into alignment. They ask us to think of ourselves as human beings first, rather than members of a special group.

The interviews give us the flavor of his overall perspective on life. We can hear him as promoting overcoming dissociation between the intrapsychic and interpersonal, the social and individual spheres of life, private and public, political, and personal. His words rung out against our being political bystanders. Fromm argued passionately for psychoanalysts' active involvement in society. In one interview, he asserts:

> Private and public life cannot be separated. We cannot split off our knowledge of ourselves from our knowledge of society. Both belong together. This is, I think, an error committed by Freud and many analysts who felt that the two things could be separated, that we could gain complete understanding of ourselves but remain blind to social processes. This just isn't so, if for no other reason than that the truth is indivisible.
>
> (pp. 115–116)

This is a ringing statement of what Fromm required of himself and what he demands of us. In effect, he is calling us out if we think we can ignore society's influence. For the love of life, we must rise to his challenge.

Note

1 Unless otherwise indicated, biographical data in this chapter is from Burston (1991), Cortina and Maccoby (1996), and Funk (2000, 2019).

References

Buechler, S. (1988). Joining the psychoanalytic culture. *Contemporary Psychoanalysis*, 24, 462–470.

Buechler, S. (1995). Hope as inspiration in psychoanalysis. *Psychoanalytic Dialogues*, 5, 63–74.

Buechler, S. (1996). A commentary. In M. Cortina & M. Maccoby (Eds), *A prophetic analyst: Erich Fromm's contribution to psychoanalysis* (pp. 402–412). Jason Aronson.

Buechler, S. (2004). *Clinical values: Emotions that guide psychoanalytic treatment*. The Analytic Press.

Buechler, S. (2008). *Making a difference in patients' lives: Emotional experience in the therapeutic setting*. Routledge.

Buechler, S. (2019). *Psychoanalytic approaches to problems in living: Addressing life's challenges in clinical practice*. Routledge.

Burston, D. (1991). *The legacy of Erich Fromm*. Harvard University Press.

Cortina, M. & Maccoby, M. (Eds) (1996). *A prophetic analyst: Erich Fromm's contribution to psychoanalysis.* Jason Aronson.

Fromm, E. (1941). *Escape from freedom.* Farrar and Rinehart.

Fromm, E. (1947). *Man for himself.* Rinehart.

Fromm, E. (1950). *Psychoanalysis and religion.* Vail-Ballou Press, Inc.

Fromm, E. (1951). *The forgotten language: An introduction to the understanding of dreams, fairytales, and myths.* Grove Press.

Fromm, E. (1955). *The sane society.* Rinehart and Winston.

Fromm, E. (1956). *The art of loving.* Harper & Row.

Fromm, E. (1968). *The revolution of hope.* Harper & Row.

Fromm, E. (1973). *The anatomy of human destructiveness.* Holt, Rinehart & Winston.

Fromm, E. (1986). In the name of life: A portrait through dialogue. In H. J. Schultz (Ed.) & R. Kimber & R. Kimber (Trans.), *For the love of life* (pp. 88–116). The Free Press.

Fromm, E. (2005). *On being human.* Continuum.

Funk, R. (2000). *Erich Fromm: His life and ideas.* Continuum.

Funk, R. (2019). *Life itself is an art: The life and work of Erich Fromm.* Bloomsbury Academic.

Izard, C. E. & Buechler, S. (1978). *Emotion expression ontogeny and cognitive attainments.* Grant application, received funding by National Science Foundation.

May, R. (1953). *Man's search for himself.* Norton.

Schachtel, E. (1959). *Metamorphosis.* Basic Books.

Sullivan, H. S. (1940). *Conceptions of modern psychiatry.* Norton.

Sullivan, H. S. (1954). *The psychiatric interview.* Norton.

Sullivan, H. S. (1956). *Clinical studies in psychiatry.* Norton.

Part III

Fromm's Legacy

Chapter 7

Fromm the Mentor[1]

In this chapter, I describe how Fromm's youthful experiences of being mentored equipped him with a template for his own mentoring of others later in his career. The profound resonance between what Fromm imbibed from some of his earliest mentors and what he, himself, later passed on to his students was discussed by Rainer Funk (1990/2023) in a lecture delivered on the topic of "Humanism in the Life and Work of Erich Fromm." About to describe Fromm's teacher, Salmon Baruch Rabinkow, Funk "…suddenly realized that these were the very words I would choose to characterize Fromm's own productive and humanistic personality with" (p. 17).

I will examine some of Fromm's statements about what he received from teachers and then describe how his own students characterized their experience with him. Finally, I will offer some ideas about what makes a mentor memorable and, sometimes, transformative.

Funk (2000) tells us that Fromm met the Russian scholar, Salman Baruch Rabinkow, when he was a student in Heidelberg. Rabinkow was strongly influenced by Habad-Hasidem, an intellectual branch of Hasidism. He was very knowledgeable about both the history of Jewish thinking and socialist revolutionaries. Among Fromm's reminiscences of his youthful experiences with Rabinkow, I find one statement to be especially telling, so I will quote it at length:

> He was a man with whom one could never, even at the first meeting, feel oneself a stranger. It was as if one were

DOI: 10.4324/9781032693521-11

continuing a conversation or relationship which had always existed. And that was necessarily so, because of his attitude. There was no polite small talk, no careful probing, no questioning appraisal of his visitor, but an immediate openness, concern, participation. I was never shy in front of Rabinkow. I do not remember a single instance in which I felt afraid of his judgment, of what he might say of this or that, that he might "judge" me; nor did he try to influence me, to tell me what to do, to admonish me. All his influence was his being, his example, although he was the last man to want to present an example. He was just himself.

(p. 54)

After quoting this passage, Funk wrote, "Many who knew Fromm describe Fromm himself in similar terms" (p. 54). I think this gets to the heart of what Erich Fromm received from his most transformative teachers and tried to pass on to his students later in his life. Reading this passage, I am impressed by Rabinkow as a model. He taught by example. He was notable for the reactions he did *not* evoke, as well as the ones he did elicit. He did not shame the young Fromm or use his power to intimidate or prove his superior knowledge. The integrity of being wholly himself was the medium through which he exerted influence. Interestingly, I think this accords with a comment Fromm made in his 1922 obituary for Rabbi Nehemia Nobel, who was also an important early influence. Fromm said that Nobel "...*lived* what he said and said only what he lived" (Funk, 2000, p. 43, italics in original). This epitomizes the integrity that I believe is a vital factor in educational as well as therapeutic professionals. For a more extensive discussion of this topic, please see the chapter in the present volume on inspiring beginning clinicians.

Rainer Funk was Erich Fromm's last research assistant and collaborator on many writing projects. In the lecture referred to above, Funk (1990/2023) pointed to many qualities that Fromm had in common with his own early mentors. One way to characterize these commonalities would be to describe a shared humanistic orientation. Fromm's mentors and Fromm, himself, evinced an urge for independence, a knowledge of the well-springs of joy, a matchless dedication and enthusiasm for teaching, compassion, respect for the freedom of others and for his own freedom, and other attributes.

To further compare the effect of Fromm's teachers on the youthful Fromm with his own effect on those he later mentored, here are sections of a passage from Funk's (2019) reminiscences of his first meetings with Fromm:

> Fromm looked at me in such a straightforward way that any attempts at polite conversation ceased abruptly and any superficial courtesies became unnecessary. Although we had only met face-to-face a few moments before, a dimension for the relationship had already emerged, one that allowed for closeness and trust, but no longer allowed for the evasion of a question or topic with clever remarks...His gaze corresponded to his way of being interested in my inner life, my soul. But there was something else about the way Fromm looked at me, spoke to me, and focused the conversation. Despite the directness and bluntness with which he approached the uncovering of my soul, I did not feel at all interrogated, cornered, judged, unmasked, or exposed.
>
> (pp. 2–4)

Later, Funk remarks that "...Fromm neither wanted nor founded a school of thought. Fromm lived and felt what he said and wrote. His own art of living sets an example" (p. 15).

Just as Fromm, himself, had experienced as a youth with Nobel and Rabinkow, when Fromm became a mentor and collaborator, his greatest impact was through his way of being wholly himself. Also, as Fromm had remarked about Rabinkow, so Funk implied about Fromm, that a significant aspect of his establishment of trust was the *absence* of the feeling of being judged or in any way shamed.

Generosity characterized some of Fromm's experiences with mentors, as well as some supervisees who reminisced about their work with Fromm. In his "Memories of Rav. Zalman Baruch Rabinkow," Fromm (1964) wrote "There was always a ready reception for his visitors and pupils, an eagerness to teach, and never an attitude which could make one feel that one took his time" (p. 1).

Similarly, commenting on Fromm as his supervisor, David Schecter (2009) said, "Fromm was most generous in his supervisory work. He shared his private associations not only through direct interpretation but through jokes, parables, and stories from his own life" (p. 74). I think *implicit* messages in this sharing may be especially significant, perhaps, in part, because they are unspoken but pervasive.

When a supervisor welcomes the mentee into their mind, it conveys a collegial bond and that the supervisor genuinely wants to communicate. It also signals that the supervisor is willing to "reach into" themselves in the interest of the supervisee's learning process. It implicitly says that there is nothing to fear from being open and straightforward. Generously sharing one's thoughts is, itself, a statement about what most matters. The mentor is, in effect, trusting that the learner will hear constructively. On a concrete level, the mentor is expressing that contributing to the mentee's education is worth their time. That all of this is expressed in actions, rather than words, may give it a more subtle impact as a (usually) non-conscious, pervasive communication.

Styles of mind sharing differ, but a generous spirit can go a long way in encouraging the learner to feel worthwhile and take themselves seriously. I think of my own experience with Ralph Crowley, MD, who was my first analytic supervisor. Many Monday mornings, at 9:00 am, I would find articles he copied for me on my chair, facing his. I took it to mean that he had given thought to my education and that my development as an analyst had significance for him. I have no doubt that this augmented its meaning to me.

A generous, generative spirit in a teacher can implicitly convey a sense of purpose to the learner. For myself, as a supervisee and, later, as a supervisor, I have had the feeling of "passing the torch." My most influential teachers had passionate beliefs that they deeply wanted to express to me. They gave of their time and of themselves. Here is the ending of the "letter" I wrote to Ralph Crowley (long after he died) to try to understand why he had such a profound effect on my development: "Aside from your wit and patience, I so deeply appreciated your eagerness to teach. You seemed to actually enjoy it, and not just tolerate it. Your attitude was contagious. Now, I love it, too" (Buechler, 2009, p. 427). I return to this letter in the chapter on inspiring beginning clinicians.

Other aspects of Fromm's experience with Rabinkow are also striking. While there may be many ways of facilitating curiosity, Fromm's (1964) reminiscences capture this aspect of Rabinkow's demeanor succinctly: "He was open to all questions of the day, and never closed his questioning mind because of any fear of going too far in his thoughts" (p. 5). Further on, Fromm remarks, "I should also add that his method in teaching was always to stimulate the activity of his pupil, and not to offer answers" (p. 5).

In a similar spirit, I find a passage in Arthur Feiner's (2009) memories of being in supervision with Fromm an interesting example of how Fromm encouraged curiosity. Feiner framed his hours with Fromm as a kind of play. Here are some statements from Feiner's memories:

> We played with what I reported, turning it one way, and then another, engendering contact—a clean, uncontaminated, reciprocal contact-serious, vivacious, and most friendly...It is in the atmosphere of play that nothing is warded off, all is considered...the willful suspension of disbelief and a willingness to look at things from all angles, as a try-on or let's see. It is however serious in its effect in addressing potential and reducing the forbidding danger of curiosity.
>
> (p. 122)

Rabinkow with Fromm, and Fromm with Feiner, facilitated curious exploration. Feiner's comments address that, through their demeanor, the mentor can detoxify curiosity for the learner. I hear this as meaning that when the teacher is unafraid to show their curiosity, the student is more likely to risk it. The learner who is openly curious is exposing something about themselves, including, perhaps, the limits of their understanding. By setting an example, the mentor is removing a potential obstacle to the full expression of curiosity.

In the chapter on inspiring beginning clinicians, I discuss how the values of a mentor can impact supervisees, so I will limit my comments here to qualities that played a particularly important role in both Fromm's own education and his later career as a mentor to others. For me, kindness tops this list. Like the patient in psychoanalysis, the mentee needs certainty that the mentor has their well-being at heart.

In keeping with this, here is one of Fromm's (1971) descriptions of Rabinkow: "He was an exceedingly kind man. I remember how often he said '...one cannot do much for anybody, but at least one can try not to hurt anyone'" (p. 2). Rabinkow's statement strikes me as beautifully expressive of his good intentions. My own belief is that, both in treatment and supervision, good intentions are most often conveyed by what we refrain from doing, even more than what we do, or what we say about what we do.

Elsewhere, I (Buechler, 2012, 2019) have written about the analyst's motivations including, hopefully, a non-narcissistic investment in the treatment. Unlike the traditional analytic neutrality as a goal, in this way of working, the analyst and patient engage in "central relatedness" (Fromm, 2009, p. 18). Analysts' motivations for this encounter are non-narcissistic in that they do not need the treatment to have any particular outcome for the sake of their own pride. But the analyst has a strong, unapologetic, at times manifest investment in the quality of the patient's life. Similarly, in supervision, non-narcissistic investment can show itself in caring to help the mentee carve out a personally resonant style, rather than feeling pressure to become the supervisor's acolyte.

In education (as in treatment), this well-meaning motivation is sometimes expressed in what is prioritized. What is more important to the teacher—making smart, theoretically sophisticated points, or establishing a free-flowing communication? How is this priority expressed? Passing up opportunities to compete, show off superior knowledge, or catch the student in a slip of the tongue or a mistake all demonstrate (rather than state) the teacher's good intentions.

My own observation is that along with kindness, good intentions, and benign priorities, the best supervision (like the best treatment) manifests *recognition of who the other is*. I think it can be so healing to be perceived accurately and so damaging to be seen inaccurately. Fromm commented on times when he felt truly understood by mentors and when he did not. For example, although he respected Alfred Weber, a university teacher and his dissertation advisor, when Weber mentioned that Fromm might have an academic career, Fromm felt this was not accurately mirroring him, and the relationship became more distant (Funk, 2000). As is frequently true with our parents, it can be extremely important to feel understood and seen by others as we see ourselves. I would suggest that this quality may often have to do with non-narcissistic investments on the part of the teacher. The mentor who does not have a need to impose their "stamp" on a supervisee is more likely to be able to truly see them.

In my own experience, in the "letter" I wrote to Ralph Crowley, my first analytic supervisor, I described how non-narcissistic supervision helps the supervisee find their own truths: "You didn't make me choose between you and what I believed was right clinically. It wasn't that we never differed. But you just let the difference hang in the air. You seemed to believe that was enough. It was" (Buechler, 2009, p. 423).

Another quality Fromm mentioned in describing his most beloved mentors was their joy, love of life, and ability to imbue a conversation with a palpable feeling of aliveness. For example, in describing Rabinkow, Fromm (1987) said "Whatever he spoke about he brought to life, whether it was ethics, the *Tanya*, problems of philosophy, or law" (pp. 1–2, italics in original).

It seems very clear from those who worked with Fromm that he, like his mentor, inspired lively conversation. For example, here is a quote from Funk's (2019) memories of his initial contacts with Fromm:

> "I never experienced a feeling of exhaustion or a decline in attentiveness. I was wide awake and on some evenings worked on my dissertation far into the night after our meeting, the hours spent with Fromm having been energizing and stimulating."

(p. 9)

In a similar vein, here are some excerpts from a paper by Leonard Feldstein (2009):

> ...Fromm was an astoundingly vital presence. His every gesture lived and resonated with his spirit...To experience Fromm, even in his eccentricities, was invariably to liberate the creative surge within oneself. Compassion, warmth, strength, and firmness radiated from him. They flowed toward you, and caught you up in their embrace...Fromm's vitality was so enormous that it had the power to spread, and by its impact, even upon a single person, to grow...His face, his voice, and his spirit illuminated physical presence are inviolable. They will never perish.
>
> (pp. 169–170)

Clearly, Fromm inspired moving tributes and profoundly influenced those he taught. In the chapter in the present volume on Fromm's potential impact on beginning clinicians, I discuss the analogy between sculpture and the education of therapists. I believe this analogy is relevant in other professions as well. Just as some sculptors describe *finding* the sculpture in the stone (rather than imposing it on the stone), I think it is part of the task of the mentor and mentee to "find" the professional in the student. That is, it is part of their shared project to cultivate the learner's creative potential by making full use of their particular inner resources. It seems to me that the atmosphere created by Fromm's mentors and, later, by Fromm himself facilitated the formulation of personally resonant, passionate professional stances. All of the statements quoted in the present chapter attest to the deep, life-long appreciation this can evoke in the student.

Note

1 Unless otherwise indicated, biographical data in this chapter is from Burston (1991), Cortina and Maccoby (1996), and Funk (2000, 2019).

References

Buechler, S. (2009). A letter to my first supervisor. *Contemporary Psychoanalysis*, 45, 422–427.

Buechler, S. (2012). *Still practicing: The heartaches and joys of a clinical career*. Routledge.

Buechler, S. (2019). *Psychoanalytic approaches to problems in living: Addressing life's challenges in clinical practice*. Routledge.

Burston, D. (1991). *The legacy of Erich Fromm*. Harvard University Press.

Cortina, M. & Maccoby, M. (Eds) (1996). *A prophetic analyst: Erich Fromm's contribution to psychoanalysis*. Jason Aronson.

Feiner, A. (2009). Now look here. In R. Funk (Ed.), *The clinical Erich Fromm: Personal accounts and papers on technique* (pp. 117–125). Rodopi.

Feldstein, L. C. (2009). Fromm's genius was in his actual presence. In R. Funk (Ed.), *The clinical Erich Fromm: Personal accounts and papers on technique* (pp. 169–170). Rodopi.

Fromm, E. (1964). *Memories of Rav*. Zalman Baruch Rabinkow (Draft). Fromm Literary Estate, Erich Fromm Institute, Tubingen.

Fromm, E. (1971). Reminiscences of Shlomo Barukh Rabinkow (Draft). In L. Jung (Ed.), *Sages and saints* (pp. 99–105). Ktav Publishing House. Erich Fromm Institute, Tubingen.

Fromm, E. (1987). *Reminiscences of Shlomo Barakh Rabinow*. Fromm Literary Estate, Erich Fromm Institute, Tubingen.

Fromm, E. (2009). Being centrally related to the patient. In R. Funk (Ed.), *The clinical Erich Fromm: Personal accounts and papers on technique* (pp. 7–39). Rodopi.

Funk, R. (1990/2023). *Humanism in the life and work of Erich Fromm*. Lecture delivered March 23, 1990, University of Heidelberg. From the Literary Estate of Erich Fromm.

Funk, R. (2000). *Erich Fromm: His life and ideas*. Continuum.

Funk, R. (Ed.) (2009). *The clinical Erich Fromm: Personal accounts and papers on technique*. Rodopi.

Funk, R. (2019). *Life itself is an art: The life and work of Erich Fromm*. Bloomsbury Academic.

Schecter, D. E. (2009). Awakening the patient. In R. Funk (Ed.), *The clinical Erich Fromm: Personal accounts and papers on technique* (pp. 73–79). Rodopi.

Chapter 8

Fromm's Capacity to Inspire Aspiring Clinicians

How does someone become a clinician? Aside from the educational process, the degrees, certificates, and licenses, how do we come to "anoint" ourselves? What is the "right stuff," and how do we come to feel we have it? For me, this process of self-appointment or self-anointment required me to recognize that my lifelong love of writing could become a love of interpreting. I could "re-purpose" aspects of myself that were already there.

In my view, the best, most growth-enhancing supervision has something in common with the art of sculpture. Some sculptors "find" the sculpture in the stone. That is, rather than impose a design on the sculpture, they mine the stone and bring forth its potential shape. So it is with psychoanalytic supervision. In truly educative supervision, both participants search for the qualities, talents, proclivities, personal strengths, life experiences, theoretical expertise, and any other aspects of the supervisee that, taken together, can inform their clinical style. Good supervisors and their supervisees "find" the clinician in the trainee. Together, they formulate what I would call the trainee's "signature style." The development of this therapeutic identity is a lifelong process begun, hopefully, in the earliest phases of training.

I believe that the goal of all education is to "educe"—that is, to bring forth the learner's potential. Doing treatment is a formidable task. It takes everything the clinician has: all our hope, perseverance, patience, stamina, courage, integrity, curiosity, playfulness, love, kindness, honesty, wisdom, and knowledge. The best supervision helps the supervisee access these qualities and

DOI: 10.4324/9781032693521-12

apply them to their clinical work. Frequently, those entering training feel as though their "other" lives as parents, dancers, poets, activists, and so on are not relevant. In contrast, Fromm encourages us to bring our whole selves to every session. I think that is the best approach.

Much of my thinking about supervision includes the idea that training should provide the learner with an "internal chorus" of helpful voices to turn to in challenging moments in sessions. This inner object is not modeled after any one supervisor or teacher but, rather, is an amalgam of all those who have contributed helpful guidance. For example, when the clinician is feeling especially lost and lonely, a phrase from a past supervisor, or an idea taken from reading, or an experience with one's own analyst, may help to contain the painful feelings. Becoming part of the supervisee's "internal chorus" means, to me, that the supervision has lasting significance. Aside from assuaging the clinician's potential loneliness, this internal object provides a resource that fosters resilience. Clinicians need to be able to "bounce back" during and after troubling sessions and over the course of days, weeks, and years of practice. The "internal chorus" is a source of the strength to do so. In supervision, we can help the trainee develop the emotional resilience to bear the many losses that are inevitable in practice. Eventually, clinicians lose every patient they ever treat. This, in itself, can be taxing emotionally. In this chapter, I spell out Erich Fromm's role as a central figure in my own "internal chorus" and how I think his work is especially suited to discovering and sculpting the beginning therapist's clinical potential.

One of the greatest challenges in clinical education is the inevitable confrontation with previously unacknowledged aspects of the self. At least in my way of thinking, in order to become a therapist, we must become aware of our own potential for thoughts, feelings, and behavior that counter how we like to see ourselves. Opening our minds to these "bad me" or "not me" (Sullivan, 1953) aspects in ourselves allows us to know more about our reactions to our patients and to empathize with a greater range of people. As suggested in Chapter 5, Fromm's teachings pave the way for seeing ourselves as containing all that is human.

What does it take to open the door to one's first patient and, simultaneously, to open one's mind and heart enough to work well? What does it take to keep opening our doors, many times a day, no matter what happened in the last session? What does it take to keep this up for decades? Each of us brings our personal histories, our patterns of defense, our conscious and less than conscious motivations, and our talents to the task. My experience as a therapist and supervisor suggests that some bring more porousness than others. That is, for some beginning clinicians, their patient's feelings and experiences seep into them and affect them strongly, while others are less easily infiltrated. Personally, I do not see either of these extremes, or the many degrees and variations of them, as "better." But I would say they are different. It is the lifelong job of the clinician to become the best therapeutic instrument they can be. The challenge is to use who we are in the service of the work. Most especially early in our careers, but, really, throughout our careers, those who get to populate our "internal choruses" can help us maximize our potential.

The educational process can be seen as a period in which teachers, supervisors, colleagues, and patients *audition* to be part of the learner's internal chorus. My own experience is that (as is also true in treatment) lasting impressions in training are often reinforced by pithy phrases. That is, Sullivan's membership in my internal chorus is solidified by memorable phrases, such as his declaration that we are all much more simply human than otherwise (Sullivan, 1954). In treatment and in supervision, a phrase can capture an idea or a meaningful moment, cohere it, and make it memorable. The novice clinician is often daunted by the sheer uncertainty, ambiguity, and responsibility of trying to fulfill their role. I respect the beginner's acute need for guidance. I have often told the story of a young man in supervision, just before his first session with a patient, tentatively knocking on my office door and, somewhat sheepishly, asking, "Dr. Buechler, when the patient arrives, what do I do?" While I do not believe in training manuals or "paint by numbers" instructions, and I do not want to oversimplify the process, I do want the novice to feel capable enough to function. I have been that novice. I still remember what it was like. I can remember years of feeling ill-equipped for doing my job, while still needing to *look* competent.

Idealizing supervisors can have a destructive effect on learners who feel themselves to be at sea, compared with supervisors who seem to know what they are doing. The novice can feel their patient would be so much better off being treated by one of their supervisors! Fromm can help us with this, through his passionate stance (Fromm, 1964, 2005, 2010) against creating idols. When we worship another as an idol (whether a political leader, teacher, supervisor, author, parent, or any other figure), we project onto the other all our own capabilities, leaving us feeling empty and insufficient. This can happen in supervision, whether or not the supervisor fosters it. In any educative process, it is vital that the learner develops greater awareness of *their own* inherent talents and potential strengths, and that these capacities are nurtured. Fromm always took a position against alienation of one's own powers, in private relationships, political, and social situations. This is fundamental in his work and can be of immense help to the novice in any field. Elsewhere, I (Buechler, 2012, 2017) have described instances of problematic supervision in which the supervisor uses the trainee as a conduit, pouring "insight" into the novice's ear, so it can be transmitted to their patient. The best the learner can then do is to become an accurate imitation of the supervisor. This can be extremely detrimental to the beginning clinician's confidence and integrity. I believe Fromm's words can inoculate us against collaborating in this harmful, dehumanizing process.

Within the field of psychoanalysis, alienation can also take the form of idolatry of a particular theory. Fromm's conceptions about idolatry and alienation have helped me understand how this can limit the creativity of clinicians in training. In my 2012 book, I (Buechler, 2012) described these pitfalls, as I believe they can affect analysts at each stage of our careers, from training, through early career, mid-career, and late career. In applying Fromm's thinking about idolatry to potential pitfalls in psychoanalytic training, I want to emphasize that it is *not* the theory itself that is responsible but, rather, the supervisor's expectation (subtle or overt) of adherence to the theory. *No* theoretical vantage point is immune to this process.

But fortunate experiences in training can help learners enter the field, define their signature treatment styles, and withstand the rigors of a clinical career. In this chapter, I name some of the basic equipment of the clinician, from my point of view, and the contribution Erich Fromm can make to the therapist's development. Elsewhere, I (Buechler, 2004) have called some of these strengths "clinical values." In another publication, I (Buechler, 2008) divided the clinical task into its cognitive, emotional, and interpersonal aspects, and explored how each can be nurtured in training. In other publications, I have examined specific strengths, such as the clinician's capacity to bear loneliness (Buechler, 1998), mourning (Buechler, 2000), shame (Buechler, 2006), and pride (Buechler, 2010). I have also studied how our hope (Buechler, 1995), joy (Buechler, 2002), and opportunities to atone (Buechler, 2008, 2009a, 2017) sometimes serve to help us keep our balance. I will not reprise all this work here but will highlight Fromm's contributions to my own clinical functioning.

The Novice Clinician's Necessities

The Sense of Purpose

Foremost, in my mind, is the need for a strong sense of the purpose of therapeutic treatment. It is meaningful to me to refer to the *sense* of purpose, rather than to any specific purpose or goal. The clinician's sense of purpose is the strongly held belief that the treatment matters, that it has the potential to enhance the patient's life, and that the quality of a life inherently matters. This fundamental attitude can function as ballast, particularly in difficult sessions. In a chapter on the importance of a sense of purpose, I (Buechler, 2004) described it as including the expectation of movement and meaningfulness. Over the subsequent years, I expanded on the concept of the clinician's sense of purpose. In my 2019 book, in the section on training, here is how I defined the clinician's sense of purpose:

[T]he unquestionable belief that treatment can alter life, can enrich a life, and that it is possible to change the past by understanding it differently. I learned this most unforgettably as a patient in my own analysis. When a patient or anyone else asks me what good treatment can do, I don't have to think on the spot. I very much believe in the idea, expressed so beautifully by Victor Frankl (1946/1985) that the one human capacity that can never be taken from us is the power to give our own meanings to our life experiences.

(Buechler, 2019, p. 206)

I carry within me Erich Fromm's essential message that our most fundamental choice is whether or not to choose life. I am reminded of a meaningful essay by David Brooks (2016). Brooks asks what can make young people tough enough to navigate today's world. Briefly, Brooks believes that all of us would be fragile without a clear sense of the purpose of our lives. To become tough, we need clarity about the role we want to play in society and the commitments we want to make to specific others. For Brooks, fragility, a seemingly psychological problem, really has a philosophical answer. The resilience of the truly tough is rooted in absolute beliefs, dedications to missions, and fervent love.

The clinician's sense of purpose is often conveyed in the willingness to work hard. I wrote extensively about this in my book *Still Practicing* (Buechler, 2012). There, I suggested that "Effort communicates the value I place on the treatment more clearly than any statement I could make" (p. 7). When we work hard to understand the other person, we are implicitly saying that expending this effort is worthwhile and, more generally, that communication matters, the right word matters, clarity matters, truth matters, treatment matters, the quality of the patient's life matters.

For me, no other writer has conveyed the human need for purpose, and the application of this to the work of the clinician, as passionately as Erich Fromm. About the human need for purpose, Fromm (2010) clearly states that having purpose is necessary in order to make sense of our lives. He also suggested that it can be a very significant aspect of the clinician's motivation, as well as the patient's. It is evident that many clinicians who suffer "burnout" have lost conviction in the value of doing treatment and the sense of purpose that made its difficulties worth bearing. Fromm's fervor about promoting life can instill passion in those entering the field. Here is how I described Fromm's influence on the clinician's sense of purpose:

> "Fromm encourages us to fight for freedom and self-actualization, in ourselves and our patients. Fully living is a goal worth striving for. We should embrace, and not escape our freedom as human beings. We are here to promote life passionately and tend our own life force."
>
> (Buechler, 2004, p. 169)

Another way I have described the clinician's sense of purpose is that it is a non-narcissistic investment in the life of the patient. We should not need to "prove ourselves" (to ourselves or anybody else) by having any particular treatment result. In other words, we should not be narcissistically invested in the treatment's outcome. But, I believe, we should care about the quality of the patient's life. The sense of purpose is a personal commitment to nurture the lives of those we treat. In a sense, the treatment itself has a life, with needs, such as regularity, and it is important that we recognize and work to fulfill these needs.

Basic Integrity

I have often said that, while we can teach beginners much of the task of doing treatment, integrity and respect and love for the truth cannot be taught. I think it can be encouraged and nurtured, but, from my point of view, at least the potential for it is a necessity in those preparing to be clinicians.

In our "post-truth" times, belief in the existence of truth, let alone its necessity, may be harder to cultivate than ever. However, to me, that does not change the need for it and its value. It is of extreme importance for the novice therapist to understand the significance of their integrity as an aspect of their preparedness for their career. Unless the patient has complete trust that the clinician means what they say, no viable treatment relationship can develop. Once again, I believe it is Erich Fromm whose writing most convincingly communicates this necessity. I am connecting two concepts here: the belief in the existence and value of truthfulness in treatment and the integrity of the practitioner. To me, they are inextricably related. On many occasions, Fromm (2009) repeated the phrase that "this is the hope for the human race, that in fact truth makes us free, as the New Testament says (John 8:32)" (p. 8). In a similar spirit, Paul Roazen (1996) said:

> But I would insist that my own hesitancies, and awareness of how illusory objectivity can be, does not in any way imply that there does not in principle have to be such a thing as truth. A permanent danger of fascism exists in the modern world, and perspectivism or moral relativism, no matter how attractive tolerance for diversity may seem, can be an invitation to the idea that might makes right. Giving up the standard of objective truth, which Fromm refused to do, can lead to deferring to whatever happens to be dominant at any time.
> (pp. 448–449)

We all know that we live in perilous times, in which valuing truth cannot be taken for granted as a universal assumption. I would argue that it is essential to treatment that the patient trust that, to the best of their ability, the clinician is expressing what they truly believe, and that their absolute integrity can be relied upon.

In integrity, our motives, words, and actions form a seamless whole. Our way of working is consistent with our values. We mean what we say and say what we mean. We behave in ways that are consonant with our stated beliefs. In contrast, when words do not match actions, we may mystify more than we clarify. It may be hard for either participant to know just what went wrong. Something did not feel right, did not click. If the discrepancy happened outside both participants' awareness, it may be impossible to unravel. At best, it is just a lost opportunity. At worst, it prevents the establishment of trust.

I have already referred to a "letter" to my first analytic supervisor, Ralph Crowley, written after he died and, eventually, published in *Contemporary Psychoanalysis* (Buechler, 2009b). I wrote about how his integrity mattered to me:

Dear Ralph (M. Crowley, MD),

I am writing to thank you for being my first analytic supervisor. I know you helped me enormously, but I wish I could figure out just how you did it. I have been trying to understand this for twenty-five years now. I am hoping that writing this letter will help me formulate what made you such an inspiring model for me...

At the memorial I spoke of your integrity. You had a consistency of word and deed. Your way of being with me was consonant with the values you were teaching. I learned something about how to be with my patient, from how you were with me...You were not flashy. Others dazzled with their keen intelligence and sharp wit. And, I admit, sometimes I was dazzled. Like so many of the young, I confused intelligence with wisdom. I was overly impressed by a razor-sharp wit. I took its failure to help me clinically as *my* failure. Like so many others, I was tempted to under-value you, because you didn't bellow. You weren't trying to be impressive. You were trying to be Ralph.

(p. 423)

In a paper, I (Buechler, 2003) wrote about my experience of my training analyst's (Rose Spiegel, MD) integrity: "Her resonance made me feel more whole. What I was hearing from her words matched what I was feeling from her actions. She had an integrity that inspired me to strive for something similar. Resonance transforms" (p. 323).

Courage

Another absolutely essential characteristic for the clinician is courage. Erich Fromm's work can serve as inspiration and guidance toward sufficient courage to face the often daunting work of the clinician.

In *Psychoanalysis and Religion* (1950), Fromm argues against clinicians becoming adjustment counselors. Becoming a Frommian "physician of the soul" (p. 65) requires therapists to be free from the need to reflexively support the values of their own cultures in the treatments they conduct. Fromm's stance against idolatry can inspire the capacity for sufficient courageous independent mindedness in the clinician.

While any walk of our lives may require our courage, I see clinical work as calling upon a special version. We start the session with our first patient of the day, not knowing what we may be about to witness, not knowing what aspects of ourselves we may have to confront. Uncertainty, confusion, and feelings of inadequacy may await us. We may have to face someone going through a situation that resembles the worst of our own personal nightmares. Have we always feared poverty, severe illness, or bereavement? Have we prayed not to confront the death of a child? Have we emotionally avoided reflecting on certain of the vulnerabilities of the human condition? Do we freeze at the thought of prolonged legal battles, endless marital or family struggles, rape and other forms of physical violence, the losses of functioning, dignity, freedom that can accompany aging, the endless reverberations of trauma, or any other forms of human suffering? The luxury of defensively avoiding thinking about these exigencies, at least until they happen, may not be available to the clinician. We never know which one we may have to help the next patient confront. For all human beings, defensively avoiding awareness of our vulnerabilities may eventually exact a price, but for clinicians, it can cost us professionally, as well as personally.

So, the clinician opens the door, not knowing what we will be called upon to witness, not knowing what it will require us to bear, not knowing what questions we may be asked, not knowing what aspects of our own characters might become engaged. Sometimes we are asked for direct help, for active participation. However we respond, is it out of defensiveness? Will later self- and mutual reflection look back at this moment as a turning point? Will it look supportive, constructive, or damaging to the patient, to their freedom and self-confidence, to their growth, to the health of the treatment? Will we, ourselves, look back with shame, with guilt, with regret?

Here is where courage comes into the picture, at least for me. Not only must we keep going, despite all of these uncertainties, but we may feel it important to be able to start sentences without

knowing where they are going. We have no rehearsal time in sessions. While, of course, we can wait for some conviction about
our responses, sometimes the spontaneity of a response feels
important and carries its own meaning. At this point, it makes
sense to me to further consider a session as, in part, a dialogue
about courage. Let's say the patient admits something for the first
time. Never having voiced this secret to any other living being,
they trust us enough to speak their secret aloud. Can we afford to
wait until we know the end of our next sentence before beginning
it? In my view, not always. Sometimes, I think, we need to meet
the patient's courage with courage of our own.

Reflecting on the clinician's courage (to the extent it can be
separated from the patient's), I think of Fromm's (2009) directive
that clinicians need to be able to "stick our necks out" (p. 36).
That is, he advised us to shortcut the treatment process, if possible, by trusting the patient to be able to hear our blunt, clear,
direct observations. I think this advice can be very helpful, especially to the beginning therapist who is tentative out of fears
about their impact.

I think courage in treatment is often contagious. An image
frequently came to mind in sessions with patients. I literally *saw* a
target and felt as though we were hitting the bullseye. This
appeared to me regardless of which of us was speaking. For me,
finding the truth was a visceral experience. I saw it and felt it. It
was often unclear who it was coming from, but it was very clear
when we hit the bullseye.

But it can be easy to mistake (and glorify) knee-jerk risk taking
as courage. Truth without tact is just "shooting from the hip." It
is not courageous because it does not evince an appreciation of
what is at stake. It is not concerned enough about its impact to
warrant being called courage. Similarly, tact without truth is
too careful to be courageous. It is too worried about its impact to
have much impact. In fact, what it can communicate is that the
truth is dangerous.

It is the responsibility of all who enter this field to become the
best clinical instruments we can be. To hone, out of our personal
equipment, the strength to face each hour with courage, with
curiosity, with integrity and, perhaps above all, with a sense of

purpose, a belief in the significance of every clinical hour. We have the honor, the privilege, and the responsibility of making a difference in a great many lives. While challenging, this is the only basis I know for finding from within our own psyches and from within the treatment relationship the clinical courage our task requires.

Curiosity

Curiosity, like the sense of purpose, integrity, and courage, is vital and vitalizing in treatment. While, hopefully, it is part of the motives for wanting to engage clinically, it can and should be nurtured in training and beyond. In parallel fashion, it is extremely important that the clinician can inspire the patient's curiosity. Evoking curiosity, which is an emotion, is a crucial goal in treatment, since it can balance and modulate the negative feelings that may arise. When we are truly curious about ourselves, we can often bear looking in the mirror, even if we do not like everything we see. I have often said to people that instead of asking, "Why the hell did I do that?" it can be more productive to ask, "I wonder why I did that?" The difference is considerable.

One of the most significant aspects of Fromm's (2010) fundamental view of human motivations is that he took it as a given that we are born curious. Rather than seeing the human being as desiring decreased stimulation, Fromm saw us as seeking it out. For me, as a former emotion researcher, I was very gratified to read this, since it comported with my work on infant development. But, as a clinician, I think it has even greater significance. Briefly, if we assume that human beings are naturally curious, we tend to inquire into reasons when it is absent, in ourselves, the patient, or both. It makes a difference for the novice therapist to enter the field with this assumption.

We can also think of curiosity in the language of the "analytic attitude" (Schafer, 1983), which can add a dimension to all our clinical and personal experience. Instead of just feeling (X), I can feel (X) and also *wonder why I am feeling it now*. This added dimension potentially changes all our life experience.

Elsewhere, I (Buechler, 2004) have described a continuum that I believe exists every moment, from one extreme, where you have a closed mind and think you already know everything, to the other extreme, where you are completely open minded and curious. How curious *we* are about the patient will have an impact *on the patient*. Do we seem to really want to get to know the patient? Do we ask questions gently, aggressively, or anxiously? Do we avoid asking questions, perhaps assuming the patient will find them intrusive? Can we find ways of being curious without being intrusive? Can we be *tactfully curious*? Can we want to know about the patient but not want to shame, expose, hurt them in any way?

To be truly healthy, to be truly alive, a person has to be curious about themselves and other people, and how life could next surprise them. To be healthy, in this view, is to want to learn from new life experiences, to want to try out being different in relationships. In treatment, I believe it is part of our job to show the patient that we can be curious about them, and about ourselves, without being hurtful.

If we enter any situation, including treatment, with absolute certainty about what will happen, with a closed mind, we may miss seeing something we did not expect to see, or we may misread what we do see. The curious person is open to new experiences, open to learning from them, and sometimes open to changing their mind about who others are and who they themselves are. The curious person can experiment with being different in relationships and try out new roles. For the curious person, life can be an adventure (at least, some of the time).

In my first book, I (Buechler, 2004) spelled out three ways the clinician can make use of our own curiosity. Briefly, we provide patients with a contrast, a catalyst, and a relational challenge. That is, by being fully curious ourselves, we contrast with any closed-mindedness the patient may have in some areas. For example, an extreme closed-mindedness would be the patient believing everything that is happening is because they are Jesus Christ. By being curious about other possibilities, we contrast with the patient's non-curious way of thinking. For example, I would often ask patients "What else could be true?"

We are catalysts by inviting the patient to join us in our way of relating so, in the session, the patient has an *actual experience* of acting differently from usual. We are relational challenges in that the patient is challenged to deal with us, with someone who functions as we do.

The value of curiosity can be demonstrated rather than verbally interpreted. In general, I would say that "interpretations" should often be made by our actions and emotions rather than by verbal statements, at least at first. That is, when we are openly curious about the patient we are, in a sense, "interpreting" that being curious is good and would be good for the patient to cultivate. Or, as another example, if we are calm, *that action is, itself, an interpretation that calm might be helpful.* Actions often "interpret" what would be valuable at a particular point. We express our values through our actions in treatment. Do we work hard to understand the patient? To express ourselves clearly? To take responsibility for our impact on the patient? To remember details about the patient's life experience? All of these silent actions are, in a sense, interpretations about what really matters.

For this to become a natural aspect of the clinician's "equipment," the novice's curiosity must not be discouraged. Once again, my assumption is that in beginning clinicians, as in all of us, curiosity is natural if it is not dampened. In *Still Practicing* (2012), I suggested some of the ways curiosity can actually be stifled in training. Very briefly, subtle (or not so subtle) shaming and competition can play roles in this unfortunate situation. I hear one of Fromm's (1994) suggestions about training as a fruitful avenue for nurturing curiosity: "The training curriculum of psychoanalysts should include the study of history, history of religion, mythology, symbolism, philosophy, that is to say all of the main products of the human mind" (p. 101).

Returning to the idea of finding the sculpture in the stone, it is our job to help those first entering the field to find (or re-find) their curiosity about themselves and their patients. How do Fromm's attitudes encourage this? Here are some passages from Funk (2019) about his first encounters with Fromm. Recall that Rainer Funk was Erich Fromm's research assistant for the last eight years of Fromm's life. These are some of Funk's earliest impressions of what it was like for him to be with Fromm:

Fromm wanted to understand my innermost being: if and what I loved, hated, valued and sought, critically assessed and rejected, what appealed to me, encouraged, stimulated, and angered me, delighted or thrilled me, what made me feel anxious or guilty, or what frightened me. He was curious about my feelings, my needs, my interests, and my passions.

(p. 3)

His gaze corresponded to his way of being interested in my inner life, my soul...He reached out to me and, through his sincere interest in what concerned me, let me sense that there was no reason to fear for myself or my inner world. Every look and every word conveyed a sense of solidarity and kindness.

(p. 4)

While (unfortunately) we will not have the opportunity to know Fromm firsthand and be affected by center-to-center encounters with him (see Chapter 5), we can read his stirring words. Once again, I quote this profound statement:

Indeed we must become aware in order to choose the good- but no awareness will help us if we have lost the capacity to be moved by the distress of another human being, by the friendly gaze of another person, by the song of a bird, by the greenness of grass.

(1964, p. 150)

A friend of mine suggested that we buy 10,000 copies of Fromm's books and give them out as a response to the problems we encounter in society today. While not practical, this idea has great appeal for me. For now, my version of this is to wish every clinician, no matter how experienced or inexperienced, would have some acquaintance with Erich Fromm's writing. I think that Fromm, more than anyone else, inspires the sense of purpose, integrity, courage, and curiosity, that the clinician must draw on, to survive, and even thrive, in a career as a therapist.

References

Brooks, D. (2016). Making modern toughness. *New York Times,* Wednesday, August 30, p. A21.

Buechler, S. (1995). Hope as inspiration in psychoanalysis. *Psychoanalytic Dialogues,* 5, 63–74.

Buechler, S. (1998). The analyst's experience of loneliness. *Contemporary Psychoanalysis,* 34, 91–105.

Buechler, S. (2000). Necessary and unnecessary losses: The analyst's mourning. *Contemporary Psychoanalysis,* 36, 77–90.

Buechler, S. (2002). Joy in the analytic encounter: A response to Biancoli. *Contemporary Psychoanalysis,* 38, 613–622.

Buechler, S. (2003). Analytic integrity. *Contemporary Psychoanalysis,* 39, 323–326.

Buechler, S. (2004). *Clinical values: Emotions that guide psychoanalytic treatment.* The Analytic Press.

Buechler, S. (2006). *The legacies of shaming psychoanalytic candidates.* Paper presented at Mt. Sinai Symposium, New York, March 4.

Buechler, S. (2008). *Making a difference in patients' lives: Emotional experience in the therapeutic setting.* Routledge.

Buechler, S. (2009a). The analyst's search for atonement. *Psychoanalytic Inquiry,* 29, 426–437.

Buechler, S. (2009b). A letter to my first analytic supervisor. *Contemporary Psychoanalysis,* 45, 422–427.

Buechler, S. (2010). Overcoming our own pride in the treatment of narcissistic patients. *International Forum of Psychoanalysis,* 19, 120–124.

Buechler, S. (2012). *Still practicing: The heartaches and joys of a clinical career.* Routledge.

Buechler, S. (2017). *Psychoanalytic reflections: Training and practice.* IPBooks.

Buechler, S. (2019). *Psychoanalytic approaches to problems in living: Addressing life's challenges in clinical practice.* Routledge.

Fromm, E. (1950). *Psychoanalysis and religion.* Vail-Ballou Press, Inc.

Fromm, E. (1964). *The heart of man: Its genius for good and evil.* Harper & Row.

Fromm, E. (1994). About the therapeutic relationship. In *The art of listening* (pp. 96–108). Continuum.

Fromm, E. (2005). *On being human.* Continuum.

Fromm, E. (2009). Being centrally related to the patient. In R. Funk (Ed.), *The clinical Erich Fromm: Personal accounts and papers on technique* (pp. 7–39). Rodopi.

Fromm, E. (2010). *The pathology of normalcy.* American Mental Health Foundation Books.

Funk, R. (2019). *Life itself is an art: The life and work of Erich Fromm.* Bloomsbury Academic.

Roazen, P. (1996). Erich Fromm's courage. In M. Cortina & M. Maccoby (Eds), *A prophetic analyst: Erich Fromm's contribution to psychoanalysis* (pp. 427–453). Jason Aronson.

Schafer, R. (1983). *The analytic attitude.* Basic Books.

Sullivan, H. S. (1953). *The interpersonal theory of psychiatry.* Norton.

Sullivan, H. S. (1954). *The psychiatric interview.* Norton.

Chapter 9

Applying Fromm's Social Criticism to Contemporary Issues

Erich Fromm spoke and wrote with urgency about our situation as human beings. Strikingly, his words in 1968 are just as pertinent now. Here is one of his most unforgettable statements:

> I would compare us with a patient on the critical list. In other words, there is the possibility, and if I let only my thinking speak, perhaps even the probability that we are headed...for the extinction of individuality, and that means for culture as we have known it. But I also believe there is a great probability that we're headed for thermonuclear war. But I think all this is not a necessity. That there is so much in a protest longing for life, awareness of what's going on, that there is a possibility to change our course. And what I mean is, it doesn't matter so much whether we go 10 miles or 100 miles in another direction; what really matters is whether we change the direction. The faster one goes in the wrong direction the faster one gets into catastrophe.
>
> (pp. 9–10)

Alienation

This concept, central to Fromm's thinking, is as relevant today as it was when he wrote about it. Fromm (2005a) links alienation in our Western society with idolatry and with Freud's concept of transference:

> A person transfers his own activities or all of what he experiences—of his power of love, of his power of thought—

DOI: 10.4324/9781032693521-13

onto an object outside himself. The object can be a person, or a thing made of wood or stone. As soon as a person has set up this transferential relatedness, he enters into relation with himself only by submitting to the object onto which he has transferred his own human functions...The more powerful an idol becomes—that is, the more I transfer on it—the poorer I become and the more I am dependent on it, since I am lost if I lose that onto which I have transferred everything that I have.

(p. 24)

Fromm goes on to describe the process in treatment of transferring one's own strengths onto the clinician, then becoming dependent on the clinician. But Fromm also applies the concept to societies that transfer their own powers to leaders who willingly embrace the role of strong saviors.

Referring to the concept of alienation as understood by Marx and Hegel, Fromm further states that alienated people have lost themselves and no longer perceive themselves as the center of their activities. Such a person has much and uses much but is little. In Fromm's words, "Modern man is controlled by the products of his own hands. He himself becomes a thing" (p. 25)

One can wonder what Fromm would make of the current culture's obsessions with technology, social media, and even AI. It is easy to imagine that Fromm would see us as even more alienated than ever. We ascribe ever more power to the products of our own invention, becoming, arguably, eventually at their mercy. We give them the ability to define us to ourselves and others. Their data about us becomes our reality. Even to ourselves, and to others, we have become the algorithms "big tech" ascribes to us.

Another statement by Fromm (1950) points us to alternatives to idolatry:

We forget that the essence of idolatry is not the worship of this or that particular idol but is a specific human attitude. This attitude may be described as the deification of things, of partial aspects of the world and man's submission to such things, in contrast to an attitude in which his life is devoted to the realization of the highest principles of life, those of love and reason, to the aim of becoming what he potentially is, a being made in the likeness of God.

(p. 118)

Can we reclaim the powers we have ascribed to today's technological wizards? This question will be with us for a long time. As Fromm (2005a) suggested, atomic weapons, products of our own making, control our destiny. He noted the adage: "Man is dead, long live the thing!" (p. 27). Fromm predicted that evil would take the form of indifference or complete alienation from life itself. As we in my country, and so many others, hand power to authoritarian leaders, do relatively little to contain climate change, and (at least in the USA) tolerate proliferating gun violence, Fromm is revealed as, sadly, prescient. Lines are increasingly blurred between reality and fantasy, truth and lies, our profiles and ourselves, trolls, bots, and human beings. Fromm's reverence for life, his fierce belief in realizing one's human potentials, his stands against all forms of alienation, can (and I believe should) guide us today.

Polarization

A charged, polarized atmosphere plagues contemporary culture. Issues are reduced in complexity, and individuals are treated as one of "us" or one of "them." This runs directly counter to Fromm's belief in our recognizing the "stranger" in ourselves. As Funk (2019) stated it, Fromm advocated seeing reality anew each time we look. This open mindedness was also advocated by Ernst Schachtel, whose book *Metamorphosis* (1959) was essential reading in my training in the Interpersonal psychoanalytic tradition. Schooled in the privileging of curiosity, I (Buechler, 2004) developed the concept of a continuum from extreme open-mindedness to extreme closed-mindedness. I posited that we are each somewhere on this continuum every moment of every day, and that we are subject to the influence of the degree of openness of others with whom we relate. On the most open-minded end, we are curious about differences between ourselves and others, novel ways of thinking, and cultures other than our own. We welcome, and not just tolerate, experiencing what is new to us. This attitude can inform our position about welcoming strangers to our shores, assuming that we may have much to learn from them, about their perspective and, through contrast, about our own. (For more on the value of curiosity, and the idea of a continuum, see Chapter 8 in this volume on inspiring beginning clinicians.)

On the opposite side of the continuum, the extreme of closed-mindedness is paranoid certainty. One version would be something like, "The cause of all my troubles is that they are poisoning my soup" or "I am being targeted because I am really Napoleon." Of course, this is psychotic, but there are many more reality-oriented versions. The person who believes any of these variants will not entertain different ways of thinking and labels individuals as either allies or enemies. Fromm (1994) described paranoid certainty in a lecture in *The Art of Listening*. There, he says that someone who is paranoid "...can speak with certainty because all his certainty depends on the fact of what he thinks, and if that's what he thinks it is true" (p. 185). No clinician finishes a career without having treated someone whose outlook (at least in some areas) is closed-minded. The threat of being branded a traitor, or at least suspected as a dangerous non-believer, can be very real in treatment. But, particularly lately, it also exists in school board meetings, family gatherings, and many other social contexts. As Funk (2019) saw it, Erich Fromm provided clear guidance on the need to welcome what at first may be strange, in other people as well as in oneself. Funk suggests that Fromm's concept of productive love included an interest in everything and openness toward the unknown. Fromm's *Beyond the Chains of Illusion* (1962) says that "The attitude toward the 'stranger' is inseparable from the attitude toward oneself. As long as any fellow being is experienced as fundamentally different from myself, as long as he remains a stranger, I remain a stranger to myself, too" (pp. 171–172).

It seems clear to me that without some curiosity, no psychological treatment could really be effective, since, by definition, the patient has to be willing to entertain new thoughts, perspectives, and, potentially, new behaviors. Change in the individual and in society depends on an adequate degree of open-mindedness. Here, again, Fromm's wisdom seems especially apt today.

I suggest that by assuming curiosity is natural, both emotion theory (Buechler, 2004; Izard, 1972, 1977) and Fromm's work tell us to look for what might be blocking it, when it is absent, rather than how to promote it. At least, this is a first step.

In treatment, open-mindedness can be modeled through the clinician's attitude toward discovering in ourselves what was previously non-conscious. In this and other interpersonal situations, it may be possible to highlight the value of new perspectives. Perhaps it can sometimes help if we believe that new ideas do not, necessarily, have to threaten old identifications. Sometimes, ways of integrating old and new ideas allay anxieties. My own work (Buechler, 2008, 2012, 2017, 2019) has developed twin approaches: the notion of "making the strange familiar" (by linking it with previously accepted ideas) and "making the familiar strange" (by questioning unrecognized assumptions). I have also suggested that an experimental spirit can be facilitative. That is, playfully introducing thought experiments might have an influence. Whenever I seemed too wedded to a particular perspective, my training analyst asked, "what else could be true?" Her question has stayed with me for many years.

Another format closed-mindedness can take is prejudice. One-dimensional labels tell the prejudiced all they feel they need to know in order to cast aspersions. Prejudice narrows vision, oversimplifying perception. It is the closed-mindedness of "us" versus "them." Fromm defined fanatic racism in *The Heart of Man: Its Genius for Good and Evil* (1964): "The essence of this overestimation of one's own position and the hate for all who differ from it is narcissism. 'We' are admirable; 'they' are despicable, 'we' are good; 'they' are evil" (p. 82). Fromm contrasts this thinking with the humanism that avers that all humankind is one, and each individual carries within all that is human.

My own work (Buechler, 2008) linked an open-minded embrace of the oneness of humankind with a potential joy. Schachtel (1959) connected joy with the feeling of being "related to all things living" (pp. 42–43). I (Buechler, 2008) suggested that the clinician is in a unique position to fully realize that nothing human is alien to us, since we encounter some of life's dilemmas in many of the sessions we conduct. We have the opportunity to grasp that, faced with the challenges of being human, many differences between people melt away. For example, in treating an adult patient whose parent has lost all memory to Alzheimer's disease and does not even recognize their daughter, whatever differences the patient and I had were dwarfed by our common humanity in the face of loss. In addition to sadness, I also felt "added to." That is, after this session, I felt I understood something more about being human, and my empathy with the patient was stronger. Recognition of this can bring warmth and a sense of connectedness along with sorrow. A closed-minded, one-dimensional approach might have categorized the patient or her feelings with an explanatory label. I think of this pigeon-holing as an easy way to distance oneself from human vulnerability. In a sense, it can be used prejudicially to divide "us" from the sufferers, "them." But, like all forms of closed-mindedness, it robs the perceiver of a nuanced picture and the fullness of feeling that can accompany connecting with the human family. On the world stage, I think the price of prejudice is too painfully obvious to catalogue. But I believe Erich Fromm would say that the toll is the same. With prejudice, societies, just as much as individuals, lose the chance to actualize our full humanity.

On a more personal note, I (Buechler, 2020a) have written about defensive patterns in me that limit my ability to connect with the suffering "other." I examined a form of polarizing alienation in myself, born of early and frequent exposure to people surviving trauma. Partially as a result, I can only bear limited forays into accounts of torture and other atrocities. In that paper, I explore the price I pay for this defensive process. I suspect I am not alone in needing to distance myself from empathic immersion in extreme pain. Fromm's views on polarizing and alienation as well as his conception of our common humanity have been crucial to my self-confrontation.

Fromm (2010) also touched on "us vs. them" thinking in his book on the pathology of normalcy. In passages about the significance of overcoming group narcissism, he examined patriotic forms it can take:

The very same attitude, that my nation is best, the most wonderful, the most this, that, or the other attitude, which would sound utterly revolting or crazy if referred to the individual or family, sounds praiseworthy, moral, and good if it is referred to a whole national group, or religion, for that matter.

(p. 90)

Fromm (1994) also described a form of collective narcissism:

When a man says, "My country is the most wonderful country, we are better than anyone else," then you can say he is patriotic, loyal, a good citizen, and nobody says he is crazy because it is shared by everybody else. Everybody else likes to feel that too, and people of another country like to feel that about their country. When the two get together there is a tremendous hate, because each has to preserve the collective narcissism in which he shares with others in the wonderful feeling of his greatness.

(p. 184)

Fromm sees this as at the bottom of most wars. I think of this as a very significant statement in our own time.

In my view, scientific advances have put us in a position to view ourselves as citizens of the world, concerned about global threats such as climate change, pandemics, income disparity, and racial discrimination. But group narcissism, like narcissism in individuals, narrows our focus, forfeiting the sense of human solidarity in order to gain an illusion of superiority, and sacrifices connection with reality. I feel sure that Fromm would be disheartened by the many contemporary movements that blindly elevate national pride over membership in a globally interdependent and connected world. In the beautiful words that ended a book that was aptly titled *The Significance of Erich Fromm for the Present*, Funk and Lechhab (2022) point to Fromm's belief that almost nothing human was strange to him, and his sense that our commonly held existential questions should unite us as human beings. They conclude that, for Fromm, "This is the true reason for his love for humanity, which characterizes a citizen of the world" (p. 101).

Integrity in Contemporary Society

Fromm identified the problem of developing and maintaining integrity in the context of his own era, but I think it is as crucial an issue in ours. In an essay entitled "What I Do Not Like About Contemporary Society" (2005b), he expressed that he felt that so many people could not really be trusted because they are, in a sense, for sale:

> [E]ver fewer people have convictions. By conviction I mean an opinion rooted in the person's character, in the total personality, and which therefore motivates action…They satisfy every need immediately, have little patience to learn, cannot easily endure frustration, and have no center within themselves, no sense of identity. They suffer from this and question themselves, their identity, and the meaning of life.
>
> (p. 39)

In an essay on "The Psychological Problem of Man in Modern Society" (2005c), Fromm discusses the commodification of human beings: "Man has transformed *himself* into a commodity and experiences his life as capital to be invested profitably" (p. 33, italics in original). Written in 1964, this essay can be applied to contemporary society. Our work lives and leisure time are devoted to consuming, which distracts us from self-contemplation. Fromm describes the result of this:

> "Man, having been transformed into a thing, is anxious, without faith, without conviction, with little capacity for love. He escapes into busy-ness, alcoholism, extreme sexual promiscuity, and psychosomatic symptoms of all kinds, which can best be explained by the theory of stress."
>
> (p. 36)

Here, Fromm is focusing on the problems this creates for the individual, but, clearly, it has a negative impact on society as a whole. Perhaps there have always been "spin doctors," adept at selling ideas, products, and even themselves. But trends have exacerbated the problem today. Social media allows us to fabricate "selves" and advertise them with impunity. What has been called our "truth decay" (Kakutani, 2018, p. 13) questions the very existence of objective reality. Along with truth, expertise has become suspect (Nichols, 2017). The result is a leveling of opinions with facts, hearsay with evidence, and science with supposition.

In sharp contrast, Fromm (2009) affirmed the existence and eternal value of truth: "...this is the hope for the human race, that in fact truth makes us free, as the New Testament says (John 8:32)" (p. 8). For a discussion of this quote, please see the chapter on inspiring beginning clinicians.

Clinically, when patients come to therapy wondering if abuse "really" happened, and whether or not their experiences were "really" bad, if the clinician is a sceptic about the existence of truth, this will surely complicate their work.

In *Psychoanalysis and Religion* (1950), Fromm commented:

> "...the practicing psychiatrist could not work were he not concerned with the truth of an idea, that is, with its relation to the phenomena it tends to portray. Otherwise, he could not speak of a delusion or a paranoid system."
>
> (p. 15)

As I read Fromm, I hear him saying that attaining objectivity is a goal we strive for through the exercise of our capacity for reason. In *Man for Himself* (1947), defining the productive character orientation, Fromm emphasized the cultivation of the power to reason, along with the capacity for love. In *The Sane Society* (1955), Fromm defined productiveness as including "...the grasp of reality inside and outside of ourselves, that is, by the development of objectivity and reason..." (p. 69).

To our contemporary ears, "the development of objectivity and reason" may sound like old-fashioned goals, but I believe they have just as much meaning today as they did when Fromm wrote them. I struggle to imagine what it is like to grow up in a post-truth world. How does the individual sort out conspiracy theories from independent minded social critics? One of the challenges is the waning of the belief in evidence itself. Andy Norman (2022), of the Humanism Initiative at Carnegie Mellon University, said, "...when people lose the 'meta belief' that beliefs should change in response to evidence, they become more susceptible to conspiracy theories, paranormal beliefs, science denial and extremism—mind viruses, if you will" (p. 49). Norman calls this the "...root cause of our post-truth predicament" (p. 49). It might be useful to speculate on how this affects the development and active functioning of reason, included in Fromm's notions of the productive orientation.

"Post-truth" challenges another aspect of personal development and societal functioning. Put simply, in our cynical contemporary world, how do we make our lives stand for something, and how do we engage with each other in fighting for societal improvement? I think that the very notion of "improvement" rests on a belief that there are enduring "truths" about what human beings need in order to live healthy lives. Making our lives stand for something and fighting together for a humanistic society were crucial to Fromm's over-arching hopes for humanity. Personally, my own therapeutic zeal and passionate hopes for the future have similar well-springs. For me, Fromm's fundamental premises only grow in significance as time goes by.

A passage from Fromm's (2005b) "What I Do Not Like in Contemporary Society" is almost surreal in its applicability to our times. I quote it at length:

> What I dislike most is summed up in the description in Greek mythology of the "Iron Race" the Greeks saw emerging. This description is—according to Hesiod's Erga (lines 132–42)—as follows: "As generations pass, they grow worse. A time will come when they have grown so wicked that they will worship power; might will be right to them and reverence for the good will cease to be. At last, when no man is angry anymore at wrongdoing or feels shame in the presence of the miserable, Zeus will destroy them too. And yet even then something might be done, if only the common people would rise and put down rulers who oppress them."
>
> (p. 40)

Where does that leave the individual and the development of belief in one's own faithfulness to truth and personal integrity? The value of truth and, more generally, the significance of integrity have been central to my own writing (Buechler, 2003, 2004). In a more recent publication, I (Buechler, 2020b) question the effect on our sense of integrity when we hold theories that emphasize personality rather than character. If we believe that we exist as personalities in varying self-states, rather than in enduring character formations, how does this impact the development of the feeling of integrity? Can we still feel cohesive and centered, if we see ourselves as having personality patterns that shift in varying relationships? I think this issue is particularly significant for the developing clinician, for whom the ability to inspire trust is key to therapeutic effectiveness. I have often said that unless the patient trusts in the fundamental integrity of the clinician no meaningful treatment can exist. But I see it as vital in every walk of life. Fromm (1955) pinpointed the difficulty maintaining wholeness in his own time:

> "It is the very evil of present-day culture that it separates and compartmentalizes the various spheres of living. The way to sanity lies in overcoming this split and in arriving at a new unification and integration within society and within the individual being."
>
> (p. 326)

It seems to me that his delineation of this problem is just as relevant today as it was when he expressed it.

Societal Disintegration

Once again, it can be startling, and even uncanny, to read Fromm's words from more than 50 years ago and realize how closely they apply to current issues. Fromm's profound understanding of forces that can tear a society apart, delivered as a lecture in 1969, could have appeared in the opinion section of my *New York Times* as I write this in 2023. The lecture was entitled "The Disintegration of Societies" (2005d), and was given in January, 1969, at a symposium of the Academia Nacional de Medicina in Mexico City. Fundamentally, Fromm explains how systems work, then goes on to outline what can lead to their disintegration. As is often the case, his penetrating mind zeroes in on the core issues, getting to the heart of what threatens the destruction of the Western world. I am tempted to quote very liberally from this astonishing essay but will confine myself to a few excerpts:

> [S]ystems disintegrate if contradictions within them become excessive, and if single parts and the system as a whole have lost the capacity for regenerative adaptation to changed circumstances.
>
> (p. 45)

> The most important contradiction perhaps is the fact that the rich nations grow richer and the poor nations relatively poorer and that no serious effort is being made to change that trend.
>
> (p. 48)

> Another contradiction lies in the drastic split between the traditional religious and humanistic values that are still generally accepted in the Western world and new technological values and norms that are their very opposites. The traditional values say that one ought to do something because it is good, true, or beautiful, or, to put it differently, because it serves the unfolding and growth of man. The new technological value says one ought to do something because it is *technically possible*.
>
> (p. 48, italics in original)

Fromm goes on to comment that in individuals, this contradiction can result in a waste of human energy, a guilty conscience, a sense of purposelessness, and an inability to deal effectively with the threat of nuclear weapons. No less than survival is at stake.

In another comment, Fromm points to the problem when literacy is more prevalent but does not lead to enhanced capacity for critical thinking. Taken together, these observations strike me as a much-needed warning. Just as an individual with directly contradictory goals can become dysfunctional, so, as a society, might we disintegrate. What I find most moving and illuminating is that Fromm's views rest on passionately held convictions about the supreme significance of enhancing human growth. To me, it is a striking example of how deeply held beliefs can guide us to greater clarity. Specific clashes between humanistic and technological/consumerist values shift over time, but the basic challenge remains. Fromm is clear about his own time and ours because his beliefs are rooted in passionate convictions about what really matters.

Continuing Relevance of the Concept of Necrophilia

In the fourth chapter of the present book, I outlined his theory of biophilia (love of life) and necrophilia (love for that which is lifeless). Our obsessive preoccupation with gadgets fits the description of today's necrophilic trade-offs. Without necessarily consciously intending it, we rely more and more on technology to think/edit/research for us. What effect is this having on the development of, for example, the ability of our children to spell, their mastery of the basics of grammar, their capacity to concentrate, and, more generally, to think critically? This can be argued endlessly, but I do not think our increasing dependence on technology can be questioned. I think Fromm would say that it is not technology itself that is the problem, but, rather, *the sacrificing of the development of our own powers.* In every chapter of this volume, Fromm's prioritizing human growth is apparent. I think of it as an outgrowth of his love for humanity. He wants us to thrive, the way a parent might want their child to become all they can be. Every time I reread his work, Fromm's passionate humanism moves and inspires me. Fromm's stance has always functioned as my compass. It does not get me (or, by analogy, us) out of the woods, but it does point the way forward.

The Crucial Balance

Much of the time when I reread Fromm, two familiar thoughts occur to me. The first is that his words are just as applicable today as when he wrote them. The second is how much my own theoretical vantage point owes to his.

This is particularly so when I read his essay "On the Common Struggle Against Idolatry" (2005e). There, he characterizes the people of his own age as "...ready to risk nuclear self-destruction because life has ceased to make sense, to be interesting, and to give joy. If this development is not stopped, nothing will prevent the nuclear catastrophe" (p. 98). Further on the same page, he draws the contrast between "...life and things, between ideas and ideologies, between the joy of living and the thrill of consuming" (p. 98)

Fromm is pointing to a crucial balance between our positive motivations to cherish and preserve life versus the forces in the other direction. Applying this to our world today, we can add climate change to the list of dangers we face. What is so striking to me, as I reread this in 2023, is that the balance between positive and negative emotional pulls has been one of the central themes of my own work (Buechler, 2004, 2008, 2012, 2019), but I arrived at this theme largely through my study of emotional development in infants (Buechler & Izard, 1980). Briefly, in research with Cal Izard, I explored the balance between positive emotions (such as interest and joy) and negative emotions (such as sadness and fear). Our work on the facial expressions of emotions in the first two years of life preoccupied me in the 1970s. After my training as a psychoanalyst, I began to make connections between this research and psychoanalytic thinking and arrived (Buechler, 2008) at the conclusion that sometimes the best approach to ameliorating suffering is through a focus on the *balance* of emotions. Emotional balance became the cornerstone of all my work since then.

I hear Fromm as warning us that if we do not cultivate and enhance our genuine joy in being alive, we might not fight hard enough to preserve life. We can apply this thinking to specific suffering individuals as well as to society as a whole. A narrow focus on the forces against life is not enough. We must pay attention to both sides of the balance. If the experience of life is not sufficiently joyful, this adds to the danger of the destructive forces. Elsewhere, I (Buechler, 2008) called joy the "universal antidote" in that I believe it is the emotion that can moderate all our negative feelings, including sadness, shame, guilt, and anger. Genuine joy in living can lift sorrow, remind us of our better qualities, and modulate aggressive impulses.

Fromm helps us distinguish between a genuine joy in living versus thrill seeking. The nature of enlivening joy has also been a central theme in my own work. Briefly, I (Buechler, 2008) distinguished two fundamental sources of joy: the potentially profound pleasure of connecting with humanity as a whole, and the equally meaningful recognition of one's individuality. Though they may sound contradictory, I believe they co-exist. They form two aspects of the joy that can undergird ongoing coping, resilience, and growth. I discuss this at much greater length in my book on emotions in treatment (Buechler, 2008). Fromm's thinking, along with Schachtel's (1959) groundbreaking work and discrete emotion theory (Izard, 1972), were crucial to the development of my own perspective. Without joy, life would be bleak. As Fromm might put it, the only way to survive in such a world is to distract oneself, with addictive behavior and/or submersion in the lure of media-obsessed, competitive consumption. But joy, curiosity, and love can help us balance our inevitable sorrows and motivate our passionate fight for life.

References

Buechler, S. (2003). Analytic integrity. *Contemporary Psychoanalysis*, 39, 323–326.

Buechler, S. (2004). *Clinical values: Emotions that guide psychoanalytic treatment*. The Analytic Press.

Buechler, S. (2008). *Making a difference in patients' lives: Emotional experience in the therapeutic setting*. Routledge.

Buechler, S. (2012). *Still practicing: The heartaches and joys of a clinical career*. Routledge.

Buechler, S. (2017). *Psychoanalytic reflections: Training and practice*. IPBooks.

Buechler, S. (2019). *Psychoanalytic approaches to problems in living: Addressing life's challenges in clinical practice*. Routledge.

Buechler, S. (2020a). Empathy with strangers: Personal reflections. *Contemporary Psychoanalysis*, 57, 446–473.

Buechler, S. (2020b). Review of character: The history of a cultural obsession. *Contemporary Psychoanalysis*, 57, 637–647.

Buechler, S. & Izard, C. E. (1980). Anxiety in childhood and adolescence. In I. Kutash & L. Schlesinger (Eds), *Pressure point: Perspectives on stress and anxiety* (pp. 285–298). Jossey-Bass.

Fromm, E. (1947). *Man for himself.* Rinehart.

Fromm, E. (1950). *Psychoanalysis and religion.* Vail-Ballou Press, Inc.

Fromm, E. (1955). *The sane society.* Henry Holt & Company.

Fromm, E. (1962). *Beyond the chains of illusion: My encounter with Marx and Freud.* Simon & Schuster.

Fromm, E. (1964). *The heart of man: Its genius for good and evil.* Harper & Row.

Fromm, E. (1968). "Is man alive?" An interview with Edwin Newman. *International Erich Fromm Society Journal*, 16, 9–10.

Fromm, E. (1994). Specific methods to cure modern character neuroses. In *The art of listening* (pp. 163–192). Continuum.

Fromm, E. (2005a). Modern man and his future. In *On being human* (pp. 15–31). Continuum.

Fromm, E. (2005b). What I do not like about contemporary society. In *On being human* (pp. 38–41). Continuum.

Fromm, E. (2005c). The psychological problem of man in modern society. In *On being human* (pp. 31–38). Continuum.

Fromm, E. (2005d). The disintegration of societies. In *On being human* (pp. 41–50). Continuum.

Fromm, E. (2005e). On the common struggle against idolatry. In *On being human* (pp. 96–104). Continuum.

Fromm, E. (2009). Being centrally related to the patient. In R. Funk (Ed.), *The clinical Erich Fromm: Personal accounts and papers on technique* (pp. 7–39). Rodopi.

Fromm, E. (2010). The concept of mental health. In *The pathology of normalcy* (pp. 81–99). American Mental Health Foundation Books.

Funk, R. (2019). *Life itself is an art: The life and work of Erich Fromm.* Bloomsbury Academic.

Funk, R. & Lechhab, H. (2022). *The significance of Erich Fromm for the present.* Zeuys Books.

Izard, C. E. (1972). *Patterns of emotion.* Academic Press.

Izard, C. E. (1977). *Human emotions.* Plenum Press.

Kakutani, M. (2018). *The death of truth.* Tim Duggan Books.

Nichols, T. (2017). *The death of expertise.* Oxford University Press.

Norman, A. (2022). The cause of American's post-truth predicament. *Scientific American*, 32 (5), pp. 48–50.

Schachtel, E. (1959). *Metamorphosis.* Basic Books.

Conclusion

My Personal Erich Fromm

My Erich Fromm brings out the best in me. He inspires me to hope, even when there is little basis for it. He evokes my passion for life and willingness to fight for it. He challenges me to live all of myself in everything I do. He coaxes me away from coasting through the day, the week, my life. He gives me purpose.

Perhaps because I have read Fromm all my adult life, reading him now reminds me of a younger Sandra Buechler. She wanted her signature style to coalesce immediately, but she knew it would take time, and she was willing to endure the process of becoming a therapeutic instrument. She (usually) accepted lonely outposts, when no one agreed or even understood her position. Taking (quite literally) a page from Fromm's book, she knew there would be times when it would be necessary to choose between standing up for her convictions and enjoying an easy fellowship with her colleagues. She knew that after elementary school most choices would be between right and even more right, rather than between right and wrong. She strove toward welcoming strangers, in herself and others.

I wish I had met Erich Fromm, but I am grateful for having channeled him through my mentors. I could often recognize their "Frommian" moments—a gleam in the eye, a vibrancy in the air. A determination to live it all. When I fought for more life, for myself or someone else, I felt Fromm's support. When I could not, I missed him.

DOI: 10.4324/9781032693521-14

My imagined Fromm was never complacent. He was my most dependable internal cheerleader. He helped me accept contradictions. I needed to have patience, and there was no time to lose. I needed to fully embrace uncertainty and, wherever possible, I needed to choose life.

Index

For Product Safety Concerns and Information please contact our EU
representative GPSR@taylorandfrancis.com Taylor & Francis Verlag GmbH,
Kaufingerstraße 24, 80331 München, Germany

Printed and bound by CPI Group (UK) Ltd, Croydon, CR0 4YY
08/06/2025
01897000-0006